Being There When It Counts

The Proceedings of the 8th Rocky Mountain Region Disaster Mental Health Conference

Cheyenne, WY November 5-7, 2009.

Edited by George W. Doherty, MS, LPC

Being There When It Counts: The Proceedings of the 8th Rocky Mountain Region Disaster Mental Health Conference

Library of Congress Cataloging-in-Publication Data

Rocky Mountain Region Disaster Mental Health Conference (8th : 2009 : Laramie, Wyo.)
Being there when it counts : the proceedings of the 8th Rocky Mountain Region Disaster Mental Health Conference, Laramie, WY, November 5-7, 2009 / edited by George W. Doherty.
p. ; cm.
Includes bibliographical references and index.
ISBN-13: 978-1-61599-039-9 (alk. paper)
ISBN-10: 1-61599-039-9 (alk. paper)
1. Disaster victims--Mental health--Congresses. 2. Disaster victims--Mental health services--Congresses. I. Doherty, George W. (George William) II. Title.
[DNLM: 1. Stress Disorders, Traumatic--therapy--Congresses. 2. Crisis Intervention--Congresses. 3. Disaster Planning--Congresses. 4. Psychotherapy, Group--Congresses. 5. Survivors--psychology--Congresses. WM 172 R684b 2010]
RC451.4.D57R63 2009a
363.34'8--dc22

2010012123

ROCKY MOUNTAIN REGION DISASTER MENTAL HEALTH INSTITUTE
PO BOX 786
LARAMIE, WY 82073-0786

http://www.rmrinstitute.org
email: rockymountain@mail2emergency.com
Phone: 307-399-4818

The Rocky Mountain Region Disaster Mental Health Institute is a 501(c)3 Non-profit Organization.

Rocky Mountain DMH Institute Press is an Imprint of:

Loving Healing Press Inc.
5145 Pontiac Trail
Ann Arbor, MI 48105
USA

www.LHPress.com
victor@LHPress.com
Tollfree 888-761-6268
Fax +1 734 663 6861

About the Photos

Front Cover

Arkansas Army National Guard (ARARNG) Sergeant First Class (SFC) Johnny K. Crafton, from the 39th Infantry Brigade, talking with a Red Cross volunteer at a Processing Center in St. Charles Parish, Louisiana (LA), during the Hurricane Katrina relief effort. (A3613)

Photographer's Name: SPC Eric D. Moore, WYARNG
Location: ST. CHARLES PARISH Date Shot: 10/13/2005
VIRIN: 051013-A-8476M-005

Back Cover (left-to-right, top-to-bottom)

Wyoming Army National Guard (WYARNG) Second Lieutenant (2LT) Ben Josephson, 960th General Support Maintenance Company (GSMC), Torrington Wyoming (WY), sang and played the guitar for employees of Harry S. Truman Middle School, as well as for Soldiers in Jefferson Parish, Louisiana (LA), during the Hurricane Katrina relief effort. (A3613)

Photographer's Name: SPC Eric D. Moore, WYARNG
Location: ST. Charles Parish Date Shot: 10/14/2005
VIRIN: 051014-A-8476M-053

U.S. Army Col. Ken Cox, Director, Office of the Chief of Engineers, Col. Tony Vesay, Vicksburg District Engineer and Larry Harper, assistant to the Commander, discussed the National Register-listed historic property with significant damage from Hurricane Katrina.

Photographer's Name: F.T. Eyre, ACOE
Location: Ocean Springs Date Shot: 12/20/2005
VIRIN: 051220-A-4952E-004

U.S. Air Force Airmen Basic Jonathan Houghton and Zachary Murray, both from 332nd Training Squadron, Keesler Air Force Base, Miss., helped repair the roof of a water-damaged home in Biloxi, Miss., Aug. 25, 2006. The Airmen participated in the effort to rebuild houses that were destroyed by Hurricane Katrina one year prior to this photo.

Photographer's Name: TSgt Cecilio M. Ricardo
Location: Biloxi Date Shot: 8/25/2006
VIRIN: 060825-F-3961R-09

U.S. Air Force personnel of the 403rd Airlift Wing departed Dobbins Air Reserve Base, Ga., to return home to Keesler Air Force Base, Miss., on Nov. 2, 2005. Unit personnel had been relocated to Dobbins as a result of devastation caused by Hurricane Katrina striking the Gulf Coast.

Photographer's Name: Mr. Donald Peek
Location: Dobbins Air Reserve Base Date Shot: 11/2/2005
VIRIN: 051102-F-3742P-001

The Rocky Mountain Region
Disaster Mental Health Institute Press
George W. Doherty (Senior Editor)
Laramie, Wyoming

Proceedings of the Rocky Mountain Region Disaster Mental Health Conference

Taking Charge in Troubled Times: Proceedings of the 5th Rocky Mountain Region Disaster Mental Health Conference (2007)

From Crisis to Recovery: Proceedings of the 6th Rocky Mountain Region Disaster Mental Health Conference (2008)

Return to Equilibrium: Proceedings of the 7th Rocky Mountain Region Disaster Mental Health Conference (2009)

Being There When It Counts: The Proceedings of the 8th Rocky Mountain Region Disaster Mental Health Conference (2010)

Disaster Mental Health Training Series

Crisis Intervention Training for Disaster Workers: An Introduction (2007)

From Crisis to Recovery Strategic Planning for Response, Resilience and Recovery (2009)

Table of Contents

Table of Contents

Acknowledgements

It takes much work to organize and present a conference, involving a lot of input and work by a number of dedicated people and co-sponsors. Unfortunately, this time around we did not receive as much support from co-sponsors as in past years. The national economy did contribute to this somewhat. However, with financial assistance from registrations and private support, we pushed on. The management and staff of the Plains Hotel in Cheyenne provided a very professional and very welcoming environment for our delegates, including Hors d'œuvres and reception in their beautiful main lobby with its old time player piano and early 1900's ambiance. Once again, our partner in travel, Enterprise Rent-a-Car provided special rates for our delegates attending the conference.

Many thanks to all Institute members for their work throughout the year in support of the conference and other trainings and to the WYO CISM NET Coordinators and Team members around the state for their ongoing responses and their attendance and support of the mission of the Institute. Finally, a really big thank-you to each one of our delegates from around the country, especially those from Mississippi who reported on and represented their state and its responses along the Mississippi Gulf Coast in the years following Katrina's intrusion. Their personal insights into the response, immediate and long-term was invaluable in understanding what happened in Mississippi, especially in Biloxi, Gulfport and Pascagoula. The willingness of all presenters to present *and* to compile their presentations into the articles in this volume to share with others made it a success. The contributions and hard work of all involved to accomplish this was superb. Again, thank-you to all involved.

George W. Doherty, MS, LPC
President
Rocky Mountain Region
Disaster Mental Health Institute

BOARD OF ADVISORS Members since 2005

BOARD OF DIRECTORS

President of Institute

George W. Doherty, MS, LPC
Laramie, WY

Board Members

David Smith
Laramie, WY

Chaplain Bob Rudichar
Campbell County Memorial Hospital
Gillette, WY

Thomas Mitchell, LPC
Torrington, WY

David King
Campbell County Emergency Manager
Gillette, WY

Sgt. Randy Hanson
Rock Springs PD
Rock Springs, WY

Stewart Anderson
Casper/Natrona County Emergency Manager
Casper, WY

Theresa Simpson
Casper/Natrona County Deputy Emergency Manager
Casper, WY

Daniel R. Bogart, MA
Florida

Foreword by the Editor

There are many challenges facing the world these days. Some are new, some are old, some have increased in intensity. We face an uncertain future. We are searching for new directions and effective leadership to guide us toward our goals. Natural and man-made disasters and critical incidents remain concerns. The concerns that people have regarding the economy, homes, jobs, retirement, ongoing military deployments, healthcare, education, environmental concerns, global warming, etc. appear to become more intense and complicated as time goes by. Fear of change, fear of the future, fear for one's security and well-being and other fears haunt us on an almost daily basis. Why are these fears prominent and what can be done to mitigate and/or overcome them?

There are changes occurring in our returning military (National Guard, Reserves, and Regular) that are affecting our total society and will continue to do so for some time. How are families impacted before, during and following deployments? What impact will the current economy have on job prospects and employment of Veterans and their families? With decreasing job prospects and lay-offs, how will this affect Veterans and the country as a whole? What are the challenges facing our returning military and their families as situations in the world change?

Critical incidents, disasters and other emergencies will continue to impact people everywhere. Wildfires in rural areas, air emergencies and disasters, weather-related events, earthquakes, floods, volcanoes, droughts, etc. all affect societies generally and individuals in particular. People affected include not just the victims directly affected, but also the responders who are there to help. What follow-up is needed for the aftermath of these events for both victims and responders? What is the role of mental health professionals in responding? How can First Responders and Mental Health Professionals plan for and help mitigate effects of disasters and critical incidents?

History can teach many lessons from the past. In looking at similar events and incidents in the past, we can learn some important ways to avoid previous mistakes, what worked and what did not work in similar situations. How can we take this information and use it effectively to address current events and to plan for our future? How can we develop realistic goals for the future of our society? How do we motivate people to reach for and accomplish future goals? Identifying problems and developing solutions is one method. However, developing plans and positive goals for the future goes a step beyond. It provides direction and a hope for something improved and better. How do we develop a positive hope and direction for the future?

How do first responders and mental health professionals plan for responding to future events and learning from past ones. Using a strategic planning approach, how do we identity potential threats, identify target populations and groups? At what point in time do we intervene and when do we use what types of crisis interventions with which identified target groups? What resources are available for which identified threats? How do we do such planning, how often, and how do we exercise such plans prior to events? Following events, how do we ensure that we learn from the events and incorporate what we learn into future planning? How do we include response, resilience, recovery and follow-up into our planning? An additional variable that is very important in responding includes cultural knowledge and sensitivity. How does one prepare to respond appropriately within a culture not one's own, whether locally, nationally, or internationally?

Disasters and critical incidents occur locally. How do local communities identify and prepare for hazards within their communities? What role does mental health prepare for and play with FEMA, Red Cross, CISM, first responders, victims, Homeland Security, Military, National Guard, families, emergency management, etc.? Shootings, wildfires, traffic accidents, hazmat spills, local flooding, severe weather, and other events impact local communities. How do we plan for and respond to these? How do communities, first responders and mental health professionals prepare and plan for response to terrorist threats? How do we deal with traumatic events and how can we help mitigate PTSD, especially among first responders and military? What are the continuing effects of traumatic events and critical incidents on children? How are individuals affected by vicarious exposure to critical incidents and traumatic events? How do we effectively plan for biological, chemical and disease hazards? For example, in the event of a health pandemic, how do we avoid overwhelming responders and facilities with the "worried well"? What is the role of mental health professionals within the Incident Command system? What is fear and how do we deal with it and lessen its effects?

The following collection of papers and presentations touch on several of these areas. Discussions at the conference itself were active and very energetic.

Linking Disaster Victims to Resources: A Case Study of Equity in Post-Katrina Crisis Counseling Referrals

Kelli R. Pribanic, M.A.

Department of Sociology, University of Wyoming
and Gulf Coast Fair Housing Center in Gulfport, Mississippi

"No learning process, vocational guidance, or therapeutic counseling can hope to see the development or realization of persons if it does not cast the individual in his or her social and national context, thereby setting forth the problem of one's authenticity as member of a group, part of a culture, citizen of a country"
—Ignacio Martín-Baró, *Writings for a Liberation Psychology*

Introduction

On August 29, 2005 the United States witnessed one of the most devastating and costly natural disasters in modern history. Hurricane Katrina contributed to an estimated 1,353 direct fatalities, 275,000 damaged or destroyed homes, and over $100 billion in damage along the Alabama, Louisiana, and Mississippi Gulf Coasts (U.S. Department of Commerce 2006). In anticipation of a mental health crisis following such wide-scale destruction and loss, state and federal agencies devoted significant human and financial resources to emergency mental health care for Katrina survivors. The operative assumption was that early, mass intervention in the immediate and short-term aftermath would help prevent and/or mitigate negative mental health outcomes in long-term recovery.

However, in the years following Katrina, data emerged revealing troubling outcomes, despite wide-scale efforts to prevent them. Nearly two and a half years after Katrina, the Hurricane Katrina Community Advisory Group reported that a mental health crisis which had begun to surface in the first year of recovery had not improved and had in fact become worse over the following year and a half (Spiegel 2007). During the two-year time period when most victims typically return to a state of pre-disaster psychological functioning, findings indicated that rates of post-traumatic stress disorder and suicidal ideation had actually doubled (Spiegel 2007). In response to what was called an invisible crisis, state and local officials called for an increase in mental healthcare in the affected Gulf region.

At least one state-sponsored outreach program had already been delivering free mental healthcare to affected residents. Since September 2005, a Crisis Counseling Program (CCP) named Mississippi Project Recovery (MPR) had begun conducting free individual and group crisis counseling encounters in Mississippi's federally declared disaster zone, with heavy emphasis placed on delivery in the three most severely impacted coastal counties. Like other CCPs, its goals included "needs assessments of affected populations, linking those populations to resources based on demonstrated need, [and] preventing further negative health outcomes" through counseling, public education and outreach, and referral (Galambos 2002:83). In Jackson, Hancock, and Harrison counties, MPR had successfully made over 366,000 individual crisis counseling encounters by the end of its duration in April 2007.

However, the persistence of post-Katrina mental health problems suggested many victims missed getting effective treatment and/or other recovery support along the way, despite wide-scale efforts by disaster relief programs like MPR. Disaster researchers with an emphasis in social vulnerability would show little surprise at these findings and would argue those victims likely represent members of very specific social groups. For decades, researchers have observed repeating, socially-defined patterns of people "falling through the cracks" of disaster recovery. The socially marginalized have been noted for a tendency to fare particularly worse in recovery due to ongoing inequities in access to disaster preparation and recovery resources. The poor, racial and ethnic minorities, women (particularly single women with children), and the elderly typically not only have fewer resources to effectively prepare for disaster, and are therefore impacted more severely, but also often receive less post-disaster assistance and suffer greater and more prolonged psychological distress as a result (Bolin 1998; Cutter, Boruff, and Shirley 2003; Cutter and Emrich 2006; Hartmand and Squires 2006; García-Acosta 2002; Oliver-Smith and Hoffman 2002; Palm 1990; Peacock and Ragsdale 1997). Disasters, they argue, tend to therefore reinforce a two-fold inequality and further marginalize the already marginalized.

The following paper asks whether or not the same phenomena occurred in Hurricane Katrina. Specifically it tests resource referrals data from MPR encounters with Mississippi Gulf Coast residents and asks whether or not the program, despite its expansive outreach, equitably linked victims to mental health and recovery resources. A social vulnerability framework is used to examine whether referrals were distributed among groups by race/ethnicity, sex, and age so as to reproduce and magnify prior inequalities and social vulnerability. Statistically significant effects are hypothesized to the disadvantage of racial and ethnic minorities, women, and the elderly, but effects are only found for race/ethnicity, and to the advantage of Asian participants. Results suggest racial and ethnic minorities were successfully targeted and met in program delivery and that cultural identification in client-victim interactions perhaps contributed to a less biased distribution when compared to past disaster responses. Findings are discussed within the data limitations and for the implications for future post-disaster mental health care programs.

Disaster Mental Health, Resources, And Conflict In Disaster

In *Disaster and Human History: Case Studies in Nature, Society, and Catastrophe,* author Benjamin Reilly (2009) notes that disaster events are an inescapable part of human existence and that navigating and adapting to them has been an ever present challenge to societies. The rapid loss of life, personal and community resources, and social support networks associated with disaster losses can be incredibly traumatic with serious implications for affected individuals' short- and long-term mental health (Crabbs and Hefron 1981). Although disaster literature indicates most victims of traumatic events experience a normal range of negative responses during the event's immediate aftermath and only roughly 8-9% usually develop PTSD in long-term recovery (Crabbs and Heffron 1981; Gittelman 2003; Norris, Friedman, Watson, Byrne, Dias, and Kaniasty 2002; Litz, Gray, Bryant, and Adler 2002; Ursano, Cerise, DeMartino, Reissman, and Shear 2006), in some cases negative symptoms are delayed and/or persist for years (Galambos 2005; Edwards 1998, Voelker 2006). Many survivors of the 1972 Buffalo Creek disaster in West Virginia, for example, demonstrated symptoms of trauma and emotional disorders as many as fourteen years after the flood (Erickson 1976; Green, Lindy, and Grace 1990).

Although these findings were attributed to a loss of a sense of community and long-term disruption to social relationships (Erickson 1976), a number of other explanatory factors generally exist for the experience of greater and more prolonged distress. Despite skepticism and lack of evidence on the efficacy of preventative treatment, it is generally assumed among mental healthcare professionals that early intervention can play at least some part in mitigating long-term negative outcomes (Lima and Gittleman 2004). Moreover, individual traits like optimism, degree of social support, and a sense of mastery in one's fate typically serve as buffering agents, while particular social traits tend to associate with negative effects (Benight and Bandura 2004; Bourque, Siegel, Kano, and Wood 2006; Edwards 1998; Fothergill 1996; Garrison, Bryant, Addy, Spurrier, Freedy, and Kilpatrick 1995; Gittelman 2004; Norris et al. 2002; Jackson and Knight 2006; Perilla, Norris, and Lavizzo 2002). For example, the poor, females, young children, elderly adults, racial and ethnic minorities, and parents, particularly single women with children and no father or husband present, are all at greater risk for experiencing greater post-disaster distress (Benight and Bandura 2004; Bourque, Siegel, Kano, and Wood 2006; Edwards 1998; Fothergill 1996; Garrison, Bryant, Addy, Spurrier, Freedy, and Kilpatrick 1995; Gittelman 2004; Norris et al. 2002; Jackson and Knight 2006; Perilla, Norris, and Lavizzo 2002).

A common denominator across all contexts of heightened risk is resource losses resulting from disaster. Greater losses can often correlate with negative mental health outcomes and accompanying exposure to chronic, secondary post-disaster stressors as individuals attempt to recover those losses (Bourque, Seigel, Kano, and Wood 2006; Edwards 1998; Hobfoll 1998; McNally 1992; Norris et al. 2002; Smith and Freedy 2000). For example, a study of Mt. St. Helens victims found that those who had more incidents of mental disorders also suffered the greatest losses (Aptekar 1994).

However, losses alone are not enough to explain variations in mental health outcomes. It is the exposure to chronic stressors and conflict as victims attempt to regain lost resources that some argue holds the highest predictive power in determining post-disaster distress. Hobfoll (1998) explains that in disaster contexts where significant personal resources were lost and replaced, "the competition for resources become major underpinnings of the stress process" (p. 61). This process is most salient in disaster because resources are especially limited and victims must compete with one another to secure resources and recover losses.

Although the initial emergency phase of disaster recovery is noted for suppressing prior social conflict and fostering a sense of social solidarity and altruism among disaster affected populations, as recovery moves into the long-term phase, pre-existing conflict is noted for re-emerging as groups compete for scarce resources (Quarantelli and Dynes 1976).

As a result, as Edwards (1998) states:

> Members of economically vulnerable and socially marginalized groups appear to be more susceptible to disaster-related stress because they are systematically denied equal access to the resources that facilitate disaster recovery for more socially privileged groups. (P. 122)

Minorities and the socially disadvantaged are not only less likely to have adequate resources, but they are also less likely to seek out and/or receive post-disaster assistance, and, therefore, often times are more likely to experience greater post-disaster distress (Edwards 1998; Jackson and Knight 2006).

Due to its historical origins in crisis management, disaster research has traditionally overlooked the socially-scripted facets of disaster phenomena. Disaster research first developed in the 1950s as a means for the U.S. government to assess how citizens and institutions might react to a nuclear attack or Cold War catastrophe (Oliver-Smith 1986; Tierney, Lindell, and Perry 2001). In what has been described as a "social jungle" image of society, people were assumed to become helpless, hysterical, and savage during contexts of rapid social change. As a result, disaster studies attempted to understand how social institutions might respond so as to maintain and/or reinstate social order (Dynes 1970; Tierney et al. 2001).

Implicit in this approach were assumptions that natural disasters are crises caused by externally imposed agents, that disruptions are only temporary, and that social institutions are responsible for suppressing conflict in disasters' aftermath (Flint and Luloff 2007; Tierney 2007). However, in recent decades researchers have begun to challenge those assumptions. Contemporary researchers have argued instead that disasters are crises caused by human-crafted vulnerabilities to environmental hazards, that disasters can be disruptive long after their impact (Erickson 1976), but more often for very specific groups of people, and that social institutions are themselves often the primary causal agents of post-disaster conflict. Human beings, contrary to popular opinion and initial academic assumptions, demonstrate a tendency to react rationally, proactively, and often altruistically in the emergency period of disaster (Dynes 1970). As previously noted, group and interpersonal conflict, as well as prolonged psychological disruptions, were found to typically only emerge after the crisis period has subsided, and usually in response to competition over scarce recovery resources (Quarantelli and Dynes 1976).

Moreover, researchers began to note that group-specific differences in material recovery could be traced by race, class, gender, and age, which seemed to reflect differences in who normally fares better in the competition for society's non-disaster material resources. These findings, along with similar findings in who fared better psychologically after disaster, suggested that sociological phenomena like class, status, and power were significant in disaster. Only recently, however, have attempts been made to conceptualize these relationships and patterns (Stallings 2002; Tierney 2007). The most meaningful and broadly encompassing of those attempts in the sociological literature has been the emergence of the social vulnerability paradigm.

The Social Vulnerability Paradigm

Vulnerability is defined as "the measure of the capacity to weather, resist, or recover from the impacts of a hazard in long-term and short-term" recovery (Mileti 1999:106). If risk describes "the probability of an event or condition occurring," and hazards are described as "the people, property, or other interests that would be subject to a given risk," social vulnerability then specifically focuses on the human component of hazard (Mileti 1999:106). It assesses the probability that certain people and communities will be impacted by a disaster event, their probability for recovering from that impact over time, and the factors contributing to these probabilities (Mileti 1999). The greatest value of the social vulnerability paradigm, however, is that it locates those contributing factors in ongoing social, political, and economic processes that displace increased risk on particular groups, therefore characterizing disaster as human-crafted and socially structured phenomena (Cutter and Emrich 2006; Mileti 1999; Tierney et al. 2001).

The social vulnerability paradigm is said to be informed by conflict theory for its emphasis, albeit implicit at times, on the role normally-occurring social conflict plays in reproducing inequality in disaster contexts. Conflict theories assert that social inequality is "neither inevitable nor functional," but rather results from "the power of dominant classes and ruling elites who impose their will on the majority" (Marger 1999:210). From this perspective, social inequality represents a byproduct of actions in the political and economic struggle for control over society's resources (Hurst 2007). In disaster research, conflict-based studies borrow from critical theory, political economy, and world-systems theory to highlight disaster victimization as "a consequence of the exercise of political power by elites and of the dynamics of the capitalist world system" (Tierney et al. 2001:19).

The social vulnerability paradigm is specifically described as conflict-based because it recognizes that disasters produce contexts where pre-existing relationships of power become especially pronounced as individual households attempt to weather losses and compete for limited and highly sought after resources (Hoffman and Oliver-Smith 2002). Disaster preparedness and recovery require that households "with differing attributes negotiate the contingencies of their unique ecological network in order to mobilize vital resources and services" (Peacock and Ragsdale 1997:26). Social vulnerability notes that the most meaningful attributes shaping how effectively households, groups, and communities are able to mobilize resources and services are the same attributes that normally shape these processes. Those attributes are socioeconomic status, defined as "a category of people who have about the same amount of income, power, and prestige," gender, and race/ethnicity, although age has also proven significant (Mileti 1999:123). Gender and race/ethnicity, however, are argued to not represent key factors in and of themselves, but to be indicators of SES and a relative lack of power, which are key factors (Mileti 1999). These relationships are further elaborated.

Findings in Social Vulnerability

Socioeconomic Status.

Although class as a structural concept embodies social relationships of power, socioeconomic status is the most useful class descriptor for individuals and families (Powell, Jeffries, Newhart, and Stiens 2006). In disaster contexts, socioeconomic status (which is also the primary proxy measurement of class in disaster vulnerability studies, see Cutter, Boruff and Shirley 2003) and pre-disaster differences in high or low SES shape differences in disaster exposure and impact. Cutter, Boruff, and Shirley (2003) state that the individual personal wealth of communities and the lack thereof loads negatively on social vulnerability and is considered to be "the primary contributor to social vulnerability as fewer individual and community resources are available, thereby making the community less resilient to the hazard impacts" (p. 251).

Spence, Lachlan, and Griffin (2007) state that "people of higher socioeconomic status are usually better prepared for disasters…than others" (p. 542). Peacock and Ragsdale (1997) note that "any area with a high concentration of disenfranchised residents…should be considered high-risk because households in these communities are unlikely to have the resources, human or material, to respond effectively to a natural disaster" (p. 24). Elliot and Pais (2006) elaborate on these points and state that "individuals and families make sense of the threats posed by environmental hazards and respond to them in ways reflective of varying social and economic resources at their disposal" (p. 296). In the example of preparing for and evacuating from Hurricane Katrina, avoiding harm's way meant that residents in the Gulf region had to have economic resources like personal transportation and money to pay for gas and hotel rooms in order to evacuate, or social resources like extended family in surrounding areas with whom they could take refuge or depend on for transportation. Those with limited social and economic resources were left with few options for evacuating, which is why the poorest New Orleans residents, many of whom had no personal transportation or financial means for seeking shelter outside of the city, were the least prepared and were forced to remain in the city and bear the brunt of Katrina's impact (Dyson 2006).

However, the case of Hurricane Katrina in New Orleans highlights another important point for SES. Pre-disaster socioeconomic differences also largely shape the degree to which groups and communities are exposed to environmental hazards. Social vulnerability is created by characteristics of natural, built, and social environments. However, what is typically less explicitly explained is that the relationship between these environments is often reciprocal. Marger (1999) asserts that the social inequality that normally results from group conflict stems from "the ability of the powerful to protect their privileges and to coerce the rest of society into accepting the stratification system" (p. 213). In terms of natural hazards, environmental justice literature has continually found that varying degrees of environmental quality and hazards correlate with social hazards. Environmental hazards are increasingly distributed by power and class, making SES a large determinant in exposure to hazards (Pellow and Brulle 2005). As Pellow and Brulle note (2005), "elites can move from polluted industrial areas to less polluted suburban neighborhoods…the poor and powerless cannot" (p. 2). As a result, the neighborhoods in which the poor tend to live and be confined to are often more likely to have greater concentrations of toxic pollutants and other environmental hazards (Pellow and Brulle 2005).

In a disaster context, the accepted system of environmental stratification enables those of higher SES to live in safer dwellings, often times in areas of less ecological vulnerability, where they are less susceptible to disaster losses, thus protecting them from the impact of disaster (Tierney et al. 2001). The poor and socially disadvantaged, on the other hand tend to live in "more vulnerable, substandard dwellings served by older, less well-maintained infrastructures" that are less able to withstand disaster (Park and Miller 2006:10). Socioeconomic status therefore affects housing quality and predisposes the socially disadvantaged to suffer higher losses from disaster impact. Kamel and Loukaitou-Sideris (2004) further explain that poor, unsustainable development practices and land uses, lower construction standards, and inadequate neighborhood infrastructures also predispose the socially disadvantaged to suffer higher disaster losses.

In sum, pre-disaster social vulnerability is not random, but is patterned based on lines of social advantage and disadvantage, lines that are very clearly drawn by socioeconomic status. Due to the intersections of persistent economic, social, and environmental inequalities, low-income groups are typically limited to living in areas where ecological vulnerability to disaster impact is greatest, while also having fewer resources to prepare for that impact (Cutter et al. 2003). The circumstances, therefore, shaping social vulnerability before disaster have very little to do with the disaster agent itself and everything to do with the implications of living in poverty in a society where socioeconomic status and personal wealth largely determine where one lives, types of housing options available, exposure to or protection from environmental hazards, and the resources at one's disposal for use in preparing for disaster events (Tierney et al. 2002).

A seamless thread also runs through pre- and post-disaster vulnerability in relation to socioeconomic status, largely because of the dependence of disaster recovery on the free market. The signing of the Disaster Relief Act of 1950 and the creation of the Federal Emergency Management Agency in 1979 aimed to institutionalize assistance provided by the federal government for post-disaster reconstruction (Dyson 2006; May 1985). However, despite the availability of government-sponsored disaster assistance, the United States still primarily depends on private, free-market mechanisms for restoring communities in the wake of natural catastrophes (Peacock and Ragsdale 1997). In what is called a *market-based recovery mode*, individual households are expected to "negotiate the relevant processes to acquire the necessary funds—whether insurance settlements, government or private loans or grants or their own resources—to use in the market place to facilitate their own recovery" (Peacock & Ragsdale 1997:26). However, post-disaster competition for scarce resources in a market that already proves unfavorable to those with lower SES has the effect of magnifying and reinforcing pre-existing economic inequalities (Peacock and Ragsdale 1997).

Park and Miller (2006) explain:

> Past resources influence the acquisition of future resources, and after a disaster, already socially isolated and oppressed populations find it incommensurately more difficult to recover....[because they]....are less likely to have savings, insurance, access to credit, friends and relatives with resources to spare, and other cushions which help people to recover from disasters. (P. 12)

The primary and fundamental component of the market-based disaster recovery model is the reliance upon private insurance payments, while low interest loans and grants available through the federal government are intended to be used as supplements, when necessary, for the uninsured or underinsured (Peacock and Ragsdale 1997). Edwards (1998) notes,

> Studies of disasters consistently show that families who have sufficient income, adequate housing, and good insurance prior to a disaster are more likely to fully recover, and to do so more quickly (p. 127).

Previous disaster studies demonstrate that "high-income households have more personal reserves to draw upon [and] they may also receive more federal disaster assistance" (Peacock and Ragsdale 1997:27). They may receive more disaster assistance because they have greater access to aid centers, are more aware of their eligibility for aid, and are, therefore, more likely to seek and receive aid (Fothergill 1996). As Fothergill, Maestas, and Darlington (2000) note in their review of disaster literature, previous disaster studies demonstrate that "Upper-middle-class [disaster] victims were more likely to know how to work through the government system, fill out forms, and maneuver within the relief system—with the result that they were more likely to receive aid" (p. 165).

However, the provision of FEMA disaster assistance is also noted for being motivated frequently more by political constituencies and interests than need, which also exaggerates vulnerability among disenfranchised communities with less economic and political capital (Garrett and Sobel 2003; Haas, Kates, and Bowden 1977; Kamel and Loukaitou-Sideris 2004; May 1985). Moreover, even when assistance and resources are provided by federal, state, and local governments, there is still evidence that lower-income groups and communities do not receive the same quantity or quality of assistance in comparison to more privileged groups and communities, largely due to the design of these programs and their eligibility requirements.

For example, a study of federal assistance provided to victims of the 1994 Northridge Earthquake in Los Angeles found that Small Business Administration loans, the largest source of post-disaster residential assistance, largely excluded low-income neighborhoods because applicants were unable to meet credit and income eligibility requirements (Kamel and Loukaitou-Sideris 2004). Owners of more valuable property, on the other hand, were more likely to receive more assistance from grants and loans than those living in lower-value properties (Kamel and Louikaitou-Sideris 2004). In conclusion, low-income households are not only less likely to have the resources necessary for preparing for disasters and more likely to live in areas of greater natural hazard in less well-maintained housing, therefore experiencing more extensive housing damage in disaster, but they are also less likely to have the post-disaster resources necessary for resiliency or to be served by and benefit from post-disaster assistance programs (Edwards 1998; Jackson and Inglehart 1995).

Race and Ethnicity

For many of the same reasons that SES as a descriptor of class is important in determining social vulnerability, race and ethnicity are key determinants in social vulnerability because race/ethnicity and low socioeconomic status are highly correlated. Powell, Jeffries, Newhart, and Stiens (2006) state, "while poverty is certainly a phenomenon that crosses racial and geographic lines, the overwhelming face of poverty in this country is urban-dwelling and African-American" (p. 69). Contemporary power-conflict theories of race describe current racial and ethnic inequality and lower SES by race as a result of government-supported historical exploitation of non-white labor by the hands of white Europeans during the sixteenth through nineteenth centuries (Feagin and Feagin 2007). The power structures that were created during this time and the resulting systematic denial of opportunities for non-whites' social and economic mobility has historically served to limit the personal resources presently available at racial and ethnic minorities' disposal, while also confining them in spatial orders where they are exposed to greater hazards.

Although racial and ethnic discrimination no longer appears as overtly as it once did during forced slavery and de jure segregation, a "new racism" is continually reproduced through "subtle, institutional, and nonracial" racially discriminatory practices (Bonilla-Silva 2003:3). For example, as Bonilla-Silva highlights (2003), one of the most prevalent sources of this modern racism is found in residential segregation. Although segregation is no longer created through direct discrimination, realtor steering and larger structural constraints in economic mobility lock racial and ethnic minorities in disenfranchised neighborhoods. The spatial isolation of minorities, particularly African Americans, operates in a manner so as to "confine blacks to a circumscribed and disadvantaged niche in the urban spatial order" (Massey and Denton 1993:317). In what is called a "clustering of America," barriers to spatial mobility become barriers to social mobility (Massey and Denton 1993:317).

In terms of social vulnerability to disaster, the clustering of black and other racial and ethnic minority members in disenfranchised social spaces also creates a crucial connection between pre- and post-disaster experiences. As Peacock & Girard (1997) note:

> Minorities, particularly Black households, are disproportionately located in poor-quality housing segregated into low-valued neighborhoods...because race and ethnicity are still important determinants of economic resources, such as income and credit, critical for obtaining housing. (P. 173)

These low-valued neighborhoods are also the sites of the gravest environmental injustices. Pellow and Brulle (2005) note that race, in conjunction with class and power, is a strong determinant in the distribution of environmental hazards, making neighborhoods with higher concentrations of racial and ethnic minorities more likely to also have greater concentrations of environmental pollutants and natural hazards

At the same time, because, as mentioned above, race and ethnicity are important determinants of economic resources, racial and ethnic minorities are less likely to have the resources necessary for preparing for disaster. Gladwin and Peacock (1997) note that in the context of disaster, economic conditions make ethnic minorities less likely to evacuate than whites, largely because they lack the economic resources necessary for doing so. For example, after Hurricane Andrew, it was found that evacuation was lowest among African Americans and Hispanics because minorities are more likely to have lower incomes, to have nonexpendable finances necessary for evacuation, and to not have access to transportation (Spence, Lachlan, and Griffin 2007). As a result, racial and ethnic minorities are not only more likely to experience greater disaster losses, but are also less likely to have the resources necessary for preparing for disaster and protecting against those losses.

In disaster recovery, racial and ethnic minorities are also less likely to have the resources necessary for repairing lost or damaged housing, which again highlights the correlation between SES and race/ethnicity. Black households have been found to be at least three times as likely as white households to not have homeowners' insurance, which, as noted previously, is the primary source of reliance for post-disaster reconstruction (Peacock and Girard 1997). However, past research indicates that even if a black household does have homeowners' insurance, this insurance is more likely to be from a lower-tier provider due to economic constraints prohibiting many black households from purchasing more costly policies with better coverage (Peacock and Girard 1997). These lower-tier providers are less likely to provide sufficient recovery funds when compared to the upper-tier providers commonly found among white households with insurance (Peacock and Girard 1997). After Hurricane Andrew, for example, 15% of insured Miami-Dade county residents received less than sufficient funds for recovery because they were insured by lower-tier providers, and this 15% was overwhelmingly black (Peacock and Girard 1997). Cuban Hispanics were also found to receive less than sufficient insurance settlements after Hurricane Andrew for the same reason (Peacock and Girard 1997).

Moreover, despite the availability of federal, non-insurance related recovery resources, racial and ethnic minorities are also less likely to seek out and receive this assistance due in part to cultural traditions, but also due to feelings of alienation from formal institutions. Fothergill, Maestas, and Darlington (2000) note in their review of disaster literature that due to low help-seeking behavior, Blacks and Hispanics were more likely to be left out of the formal aid network and to recover more slowly as a result. Cultural traditions and preferences are partly responsible for minorities' reluctance to seek assistance. For example, a 1956 study of flooded communities along the Mexican and U.S. borders in Texas revealed that Mexican victims refused aid because they preferred to rely on family and kin whom they trusted more than authorities (Aptekar 1994). American victims reported relying less on kin and more on authorities whom they trusted to give them reliable information and unbiased help (Aptekar 1994). Edwards states, "cultural traditions [like familism] and value systems that stress self-reliance and self-help may prevent some groups [particularly Latinos] from participating in the formal disaster aid network" (1998:122). These same cultural traditions might also prevent groups from seeking help informally from their family members and friends. For example, although both Latinos and African Americans are noted for typically having large and extensive social networks, they are less likely to utilize the support available to them through those networks (Kaniasty and Norris 2000).

However, the most important point that remains crucial for a discussion of social conflict, vulnerability, and disaster recovery is that many minorities, as a result of discrimination and the daily stress associated with living as a marginalized member of society, report feeling significant institutional mistrust, which has the effect of preventing them from seeking help from formal relief providers. Kaniasty and Norris (2000) describe African Americans in particular as typically being mistrustful of relief agencies staffed largely by whites as a result of perceived daily discrimination by whites. This same institutional mistrust expands to Latinos as well. For example, after Hurricane Andrew, tent cities opened by the U.S. military in Miami-Dade County had very low occupancy rates of Hispanics, which were largely attributed to fear of immigration officials by undocumented workers (Fothergill, Maestas, and Darlington 2000:165). Hispanics, therefore, have largely been identified as "chronic underutilizers" (Kaniasty and Norris 2000:549).

Moreover, cultural ambivalence and insensitivity among providers is also responsible for preventing many racial and ethnic minorities from seeking formal help. Edwards states, "Due to institutionalized ignorance of and insensitivity toward the preferences, needs, and special circumstances of ethnic minority families, these groups tend to be more mistrustful than whites to formal institutions" (1998:122). For example, many emergency relief agencies have few or no bilingual personnel for communicating with Spanish speaking survivors and even less bilingual personnel for Asian survivors (Fothergill, Maestas, and Darlington 2000). As a result, post-disaster services tend to be underutilized and less effective among racial and ethnic minority groups, particularly among non-English speakers (Edwards 1998).

Even when racial and ethnic minorities do seek help, however, they report receiving less support, particularly among Latinos (Kaniasty and Norris 2000). Fothergill, Maestas, and Darlington (2000) note, "Interactions between relief personnel and racial and ethnic communities play out the pre-existing social problems and structural stratification" (p. 163). They cite examples from Florida's Hurricane Andrew in 1992 and California's 1987 Whittier Narrows Earthquake and 1989 Loma Prieta earthquake in which information relayed to ethnic communities was incorrect, racist comments were made by Anglo volunteers, and disaster management personnel focused more heavily on the needs of white communities, reinforcing pre-existing social wedges between majority and minority groups (Fothergill, Maestas, and Darlington 2000).

For example, after Hurricane Frederick, they state, "response workers restored power in black areas only after it was restored in white areas, and black communities received less emergency shelter, ice, food and assistance" (Fothergill, Maestas, and Darlington 2000:163). After Hurricane Hugo, blacks also reported receiving less support than whites (Kaniasty and Norris 2000). Black victims "consistently received less tangible, informational, and emotional help than equally affected victims who were white" (Kaniasty and Norris 2000:553). In addition, after the 1994 Northridge earthquake in California, Bolin and Stanford (1998) found that FEMA and Small Business Administration loans were noted as being less accessible to ethnic-minority households, for the same credit and income eligibility requirements mentioned previously by Kamel and Loukaitou-Sideris (2004) in the discussion of SES and post-disaster vulnerability.

These racially discriminatory practices in the provision of post-disaster support has the effect of not only reinforcing social vulnerability by denying racial and ethnic minorities access to proper support and resources, but also potentially exacerbates feelings of discrimination and institutional mistrust, further alienating racial and ethnic minorities from seeking help in future disasters from formal aid networks. Due to noted discrimination in the design and delivery of post-disaster assistance programs, daily discrimination contributing to feelings of institutional mistrust, limited economic resources and the underutilization of social resources, pre-disaster social vulnerability is typically magnified and made worse in post-disaster contexts. As a result, "communities of color are more likely to experience a decline in their standard of living than white communities in the long term (Fothergill, Maestas, and Darlington 2000:166-67).

Sex

Lindsey (1997) notes that contemporary conflict theory can be applied to gender stratification in terms of understanding how male advantage over women affords them a superior social position, both in economic and family contexts, in the struggle for control over scarce resources. For the same reasons that one cannot talk about race and ethnicity without also discussing SES, gender and disaster cannot be discussed without also acknowledging low-income female households and gender inequality's consequences for disaster impact and recovery. Fothergill (1996) explains that women disproportionately live in poverty and lower SES often leaves women with greater exposure to risk and hazards. Gender divides affect housing options, placing women, particularly female headed households with children and no partner present, at greater ecological risk.

Enarson and Morrow (1997) state:

> In general, women living without partners are less likely to have the resources—money, transportation, and labor—to complete disaster preparations. Thus, their unprotected homes tend to sustain high levels of damage. Single women, particularly widows and mothers of young children, are especially vulnerable if they lack nearby kin. (P. 120

Additionally,

> "Most public housing residents, residents of mobile homes, renters and those lacking insurance are women—often women heading households on their own income alone" (Enarson 2006:2).

In addition, women also tend to be more vulnerable to disaster impact due to family care responsibilities and housing. Fothergill notes,

> "Several studies disclose that women, as a result of care giving, are at greater risk in many disaster situations, as they must stay with, assist, and protect, and nurture family members" (Fothergill 1996:14).

Disaster impact, therefore, tends to be a gendered experience because women often face greater vulnerability to disaster impact.

Women's ability to effectively respond to disaster also reflects their general positions in a society where men dominate economic, social, and political processes and resources. Due to sector-specific employment and lower wages, women, particularly women of color, are more socially vulnerable to disaster because they tend to have fewer resources at their disposal and a more difficult time securing necessary resources in the recovery phase (Cutter et al. 2003; Lott 2007). Women also have less insurance and less savings, and, therefore, face less likelihood of a full recovery (Fothergill 1996).

As Shaw (1989) states,

> "In any society in which elaborate gender domains are constructed, then both hazards and relief measures will be 'gendered' with different consequences for men and women"(p. 13).

Disasters, therefore, "are a time and place where gender inequality is maintained and reproduced" (Fothergill 1996:23).

For example, Lott (2007) cites that 57% of households with the most serious needs after disaster are headed by women, largely because they do not have the resources, human, financial, or material, to repair their homes or regain lost resources. At the same time, those needs are often exploited by unscrupulous residential construction contractors, as demonstrated by frequent reports after Hurricane Andrew of contractors targeting and exploiting single women in Miami-Dade County by manipulating them into signing hasty home repair contracts, not completing repairs, and then skipping town with deposits in hand (Enarson and Morrow 1997). Women's relative deprivation in pre-and post-disaster resources and the conditions in which those limited resources are taken advantage of by contractors remain two faces of the same social animal: a patriarchal society where competition for resources is dominated and exploited by men, leaving women at greater vulnerability with less likelihood of resiliency in disaster recovery.

However, the social spaces and roles that women assume could also potentially serve as a benefit in post-disaster recovery. Female socialization as caretakers and nurturers often helps to mitigate women's post-disaster vulnerability through help-seeking behavior. As Fothergill (1996) explains, in comparison to racial and ethnic minorities, women as a social group are more likely to seek out both formal and informal help and post-disaster assistance for their families, which might serve to buffer a certain degree of risk associated with women's vulnerability in recovery. For women of color, help-seeking behavior is less clear because the same factor of institutional mistrust that is known for preventing racial and ethnic minorities from participating in the formal disaster aid network might also prevent women of color from seeking formal help.

Age

Age is considered a factor of social vulnerability namely due to elderly persons and children, who represent a special needs population (Cutter et al. 2006). Age becomes significant in disaster because extremes on either end of the age spectrum affect movement out of harm's way (Cutter et al. 2006:246). For elderly adults in particular, those who lack mobility or face difficulty in mobility are forced to place the burden of their care in disaster evacuation and recovery on family members, health professionals, or other caregivers (Cutter et al. 2006). At the same time, research notes that even older persons who are not impaired or constrained in mobility nonetheless tend to be more reluctant to evacuate before disaster, which can result in greater exposure to disaster impact (Morrow 1999). Moreover, they are also more likely to lack the physical and/or economic resources required for resiliency, even if they are not necessarily of lower socioeconomic status, and are generally assumed to need more post-disaster assistance (Gladwin and Peacock 1997; Morrow 1999). However, the social vulnerability of elderly persons and children is due less, in fact very little, to structures of inequality and ongoing social conflict and more appropriately reflects general limitations in resources and self-sufficiency posed by life stages. As a result, race, class, and gender are considered the primary factors of social vulnerability in disaster research (Cutter and Emrich 2006).

Summary

In light of findings in social vulnerability studies, the Crisis Counseling Program (CCP) framework, and particularly its function of referral, could be of unique instrumental value in mitigating social conflict, inequality, and vulnerability in disaster recovery. By actively engaging in outreach service that links socially vulnerable victims to needed recovery resources, CCPs have the opportunity, at least hypothetically, to diminish the effects of previous barriers to resources and create a more level playing field in the competition for recovery resources. If referrals are accepted, used, and result in acquired resources, CCPs can effectively bridge gaps in access to resources, therefore facilitating overall recovery from disaster and reducing social vulnerability. As a result, CCPs also have the opportunity to reduce mental health vulnerability because exposure to the chronic daily stressors associated with resource losses, which studies argue hold the highest predictive value for post-disaster distress, is also reduced (Edwards 1998; Laube and Murphy 1985; Lott 2007; Pavkoy, Lewis, and Lyons 1989). These assumptions are in fact the guiding principles of the CCP framework.

However, the CCP framework can also provide another space where social conflict might be expressed and recreated in disaster. Cultural insensitivities or general lack of multicultural competence by relief workers are noted for creating "we-they" dichotomies in interactions with disaster victims (Kleiner, Green, and Nylander 2007).

As Tierney, Lindell, and Perry (2007) also note,

> "organizations have a tendency to react to conflicts with disaster victims by defining the victims themselves as the problem, when in fact it may be their own activities that are the source of difficulty" (p. 105).

As a result, crisis counseling staff must be conscious of behavior that might produce those dichotomies in their interactions with victims (Kleiner, Green, and Nylander 2007). They must exercise special reflexivity so that their own worldviews, class-based assumptions, and learned attitudes do not negatively affect the care they provide. Particularly in an outreach format where relief workers and victims encountered likely represent a diverse cross-section of demographic backgrounds, a critical awareness of social vulnerability is required for ensuring that resources are distributed without bias and a magnification of prior vulnerabilities and inequalities is avoided.

Although MPR data cannot explicitly reveal to what degree its program staff possessed and utilized a critical, reflexive awareness of social vulnerability, it can look for evidence in the equity of its referrals distribution. Referrals distribution data are essentially the record of relief worker-victim interactions and are the closest available measurement of the outcomes of those interactions. If desired CCP outcomes include mitigating social vulnerability by linking vulnerable disaster victims to resources, the referral component of crisis encounters serves as a crucial step in achieving those outcomes. The equity of MPR referrals distribution should therefore be tested and used as a case study for examining how prior inequalities can be reproduced in the delivery of post-disaster assistance.

Hypotheses and Methods

The data of study were collected through Mississippi Project Recovery (MPR), which was funded and organized by the Federal Emergency Management Agency (FEMA) and Mississippi Substance Abuse and Mental Health Agency (MSAMHA) from September 2005 through April 2007. The purpose of the program was to deliver emergency mental healthcare to residents affected by Hurricane Katrina in Mississippi. Program goals were defined by the Crisis Counseling Assistance and Training Program, or the Crisis Counseling Program (CCP), and sought to specifically assess individuals' vulnerability to developing Post-Traumatic Stress Disorder, as well as to provide immediate on-site care and referral to other supportive resources. The program service area included all counties in the FEMA-designated Hurricane Katrina Disaster Zone, which encompassed 42 of Mississippi's 84 counties.

Services included individual and group crisis counseling, dissemination of information on post-disaster mental health responses and counseling services offered by MPR and other mental healthcare programs, as well as referral to mental health or substance abuse treatment and general disaster recovery and/or other needed resources. Services were delivered through geographically strategized outreach at residents' personal dwellings, disaster information and community centers, schools, and workplaces. Local mental health and human services professionals who were working in the area prior to Katrina were employed when possible so as to increase the overall local involvement and expertise of staff. Outreach staff was also comprised of local residents with no previous experience in mental healthcare, but who had also been impacted by Hurricane Katrina and were therefore in need of employment and able to utilize local competencies in outreach. Licensed mental healthcare professionals trained all previously untrained staff members to deliver crisis counseling.

Outreach was conducted in an anonymous *encounter* format defined as "an interaction that lasts at least 15 minutes and involves participant disclosure" (The National Center for PTSD, 2006: 9). Program staff recruited residents to voluntarily participate in encounters where information could be shared about their disaster experiences, how they were personally impacted, and what hardships they were currently facing as a result. Staff members were instructed to use active listening and the program's standardized log of response variables as tools for guiding questions and engaging participants in self-disclosure.

Based on the information revealed by participants and the assessments simultaneously made by the MPR staff member conducting the encounter, on-site counseling and referrals could be provided to participants. Referrals were meant to facilitate successful coping by linking victims to resources that would mitigate participants' demonstrated risk for developing PTSD or other negative mental health outcomes. At each encounter's end, MPR staff members recorded response variables observed during the interview, including indicators of risk and the referrals distributed as a result, and returned the log to MPR for inclusion in its central database. Other response variables include the date, location, duration, and type of encounter (1st, 2nd, 3rd, etc.), the zip code in which the encounter occurred, demographic variables related to race, sex, age, parental status, language spoken, and whether or not a referral was accepted when given. No personally identifiable information was recorded, which made repeat visits by MPR counselors random and follow-up on referrals use impossible.

Data reflect information gathered only through individual encounters and recorded on the Individual Crisis Counseling Services Encounter Log Form. One form represents one individual interviewed and each case in the complete dataset represents data collected during an individual encounter. Although data were gathered in forty-two Mississippi counties, data for analyses represent encounters that occurred in the three coastal counties hit hardest by Hurricane Katrina: Jackson, Hancock, and Harrison (N = 366,646). Additionally, because Katrina's storm surge and associated flooding caused the most significant and widespread damage, data was selected from only those zip codes incorporated in the MEMA Surge Map and directly exposed to the Gulf of Mexico. This region experienced the greatest destruction and therefore faced the greatest resources needs in recovery.

The population of study is post-Katrina residents of coastal Mississippi and the sample population consists of those residents who participated in at least one MPR encounter in the designated geographic area. Due to the anonymity of encounters, only cases marked as "1st time visit" were selected to eliminate potential but undetectable overlap caused by multiple encounters. After selecting cases based on these criteria, the total sample comprised 101,530 cases and a random 1% sample was extracted from the larger sample. If socially marginalized groups and communities do in fact tend to receive lesser quantities and quality of post-disaster assistance, statistically significant group differences are expected to be found in the number and type of referrals distributed by MPR employees. Differences are expected to follow lines of previous social vulnerability so that variables of gender, race/ethnicity, and age would become significant predictors of referrals outcomes. Referrals means are compared between groups using one-way ANOVA and independent samples t-tests.

Variables

Referrals. Referrals could vary in number and type depending on the encounter. On encounter logs, referrals responses were coded 1 or 0 for each type of referral. Responses indicated whether "yes," the individual was provided a referral (1) in that category or "no," he or she was not (0). Types of referrals include other *crisis counseling services, other disaster services (e.g., FEMA loans, housing), mental health treatment, substance abuse treatment,* and *other services* (see Table 1.1 below for frequency distributions). Details of referrals to *other services* were hand-written after the category was marked with a 1 or 0 and hand-written data was entered as string data not represented by values. All other types were denoted by a 1 or 0 and multiple types of referrals could be provided in one encounter.

The dependent variable *total referrals* represents a referral index measured at the interval level as the total number of referrals given to an individual. The variable was computed by combining scores for all referral categories. The dependent variables *expressive referrals* and *instrumental referrals* measure at the interval level the number of referrals given by type. *Expressive referrals* represent those aimed at meeting expressive needs through socioemotional services and support (Kreps, 1984). The *expressive referrals* variable was computed by combining scores for *other crisis counseling, mental health treatment,* and *substance abuse treatment*. Scores range from 0 to 6 and indicate participants could have received as many as six referrals to expressive resources.

Instrumental referrals represent referrals to instrumental resources like "food, clothing, shelter, financial support" (Kreps 1984:318). The *instrumental referrals* variable was computed by combining scores for *other disaster services (e.g., FEMA loans, housing)* and *other services*. Frequency distributions of the string data used to signify *other services* revealed referrals to religious, non-profit, and disaster relief organizations like the American Red Cross offering specific, tangible resources and to formal, government-sponsored programs like the Small Business Administration (SBA) and Section 8 housing program. Data were extremely varied and specific with no one organization or resource representing a significant portion of *other services* referrals. However, a consistent theme among these referrals was the instrumentality of the resources potentially offered through the referral organizations. Therefore, scores for *other services* were combined with the *other disaster services (e.g., FEMA loans, housing)* because both referral categories were meant to link residents to instrumental resources. Scores range from 0 to 3 and indicate participants could have received as many as three referrals to instrumental resources.

Instrumental referrals are valued as the preferred referral type for the potential links they create between disaster victims and tangible assistance. Considering the role access to material resources plays in also mitigating negative post-disaster mental health outcomes, *instrumental referrals* are believed to offer access to resources that offer both instrumental and expressive support. *Expressive referrals,* on the other hand, only offer access to expressive support.

Race/Ethnicity. *Race/ethnicity* categories listed on the Individual Crisis Counseling Encounter Log Form were White, Black, Latino, Asian, Native American, and Pacific Islander. A score of 1 signifies a "yes" response that the individual was perceived by the counselor to be of that particular racial/ethnic category. A score of 0 indicates that the individual was not perceived to be of that racial category. Each category was marked with either a 1 or 0. The majority of participants were White (68%), followed by Black (27%), Asian (2.6%) and Latino (1%). Latino, Native American, and Pacific Islander represented 1% or less of the total sample and were therefore excluded from analyses.

Sex. The individual's sex was marked as separate male or female categories with 1 for "yes" and 0 for "no" in each category. As could be expected, females represented the greater portion of the full sample (58%). Males comprised forty-two percent of the sample.

Age. Age was measured at the nominal level as string data and was indicated by 6 categories: Age 1 (0-4), Age 2 (5-10), Age 3 (11-17), Age 4 (18-39), Age 5 (40-64), and Age 6 (65+). The most frequent age group was 40-64 years of age (51%), followed by 18-39 (31%) and 65+ (17%). Cases from individuals with ages ranging from categories 1 through 3 represented a combined percentage less than 1% of the total sample and were therefore omitted from analyses.

Hypotheses

Where X_1 = *race/ethnicity*, statistically significant group differences are expected in the average amount of total and specific types of referrals distributed between White (μ_1), Black (μ_2), and Asian (μ_3) participants. White participants are hypothesized to demonstrate higher group means for *total* and *instrumental referrals* when compared to Black and Asian participants, who are hypothesized to have received more *expressive referrals*. Asian participants are also hypothesized to demonstrate lower group means for *expressive referrals* when compared to Black participants due to potential language barriers in communicating needs.

Where X_2 = *sex*, statistically significant group differences are expected in mean referrals between females (μ_1) and males (μ_2). Hypotheses predict that given the proactive role women tend to take in expressing needs and seeking help as caregivers for their families, females will demonstrate higher group means for *total referrals* when compared to males. However, when observed by type, women are hypothesized to show higher means for *expressive referrals* and men higher means for *instrumental referrals*, despite vulnerability research suggesting men could often benefit from use of more expressive resources and women from more instrumental. Although women, particularly in female-headed households with children present, demonstrate greater vulnerability in disaster, it is hypothesized that gender differences actually served as an advantage for receiving more *expressive referrals*, but at the cost of *instrumental referrals*. Social inequality will have been reproduced and magnified if females demonstrate statistically significant lower group means for instrumental referrals.

Where X_3= *age*, statistically significant group differences in means are expected between participants ages 18-39 (μ_1), 40-64 (μ_2), and 65 and older (μ_3). Participants ages 65 and older are expected to demonstrate the lowest group means for all referrals given findings from vulnerability research that indicate the needs of the elderly are often neglected in disaster. No direction is hypothesized for differences between participants ages 18-39 and 40-64. Table 1 below summarizes hypotheses for all significance tests for comparisons of means.

Table 1. Summary of Hypotheses Comparisons of Means

Variable	Hypotheses
X_1	Ho: $\mu_1 = \mu_2 = \mu_3$ Ha: $\mu_1 \neq \mu_2 \neq \mu_3$ Ha: $\mu_1 > \mu_2, \mu_3$ Ha: $\mu_2 > \mu_3$
X_2	Ho: $\mu_1 = \mu_2$ Ha: $\mu_1 \neq \mu_2$ Ha: $\mu_1 > \mu_2$ Ha: $\mu_2 > \mu_1$
X_3	Ho: $\mu_1 = \mu_2 = \mu_3$ Ha: $\mu_1 \neq \mu_2 \neq \mu_3$ Ha: $\mu_3 < \mu_2, \mu_3$

Findings

Bivariate relationships between dependent and independent variables indicate *race/ethnicity* is the only variable correlated with statistical significance to *total referrals,* $r(935) = 0.94$, $p < .01$, *expressive referrals,* $r(935) = 0.84$, $p < .01$, and *instrumental referrals,* $r(935) = .091$, $p < .01$, although the relationship is fairly weak. Findings from one-way ANOVA and independent samples t-tests indicate that statistically significant differences exist in referrals only for *race/ethnicity*. No significant differences resulted from *sex* t-tests for any dependent variable. Likewise, no significant differences are reported from ANOVA tests for age. Null hypotheses are therefore accepted and equal variances are assumed in all dependent variable means between groups by *sex* and *age*.

Statistically significant differences did exist for *race/ethnicity* in *total referrals,* $F(3, 933) = 7.45$, $p < .001$, *expressive referrals,* $F(3, 933) = 4.28$, $p < .01$, and *instrumental referrals,* $F(3, 933) = 4.93$, $p < .01$. However, although initial null hypotheses of no difference can be rejected, more detailed LSD Post Hoc comparisons reveal directions unanticipated in alternative hypotheses. Statistically significant differences favoring Asians were found in combinations with both Black and White participants (see Appendix 6). When comparing means for each dependent variable, Asian participants show a higher average number of *total referrals* ($M = 1.12$, $SD = 0.74$), *expressive referrals* ($M = 0.6$, $SD = .81$), and *instrumental referrals* ($M = 1.04$, $SD = 0.54$) when compared to their Black and White counterparts. White participants, on average, did not, as was hypothesized, receive more *total* or *instrumental referrals* than Black or Asian participants, nor did Black participants show a higher mean average for *expressive referrals* when compared to Asian participants. Null hypotheses fail to be rejected for the Black-White comparison while those involving Asian participants are rejected. Directions of alternative hypotheses are, however, not supported.

Discussion

Mississippi Project Recovery data show a number of expected and unexpected relationships. Findings of no difference in referrals are of greater surprise for *sex* than they are for *age*. Although the elderly are especially vulnerable in disaster, because their vulnerability lies more in limited self-sufficiency rather than in a history of oppression, it is not believed that findings of no difference indicate a discriminatory or neglectful referrals distribution that would have magnified vulnerability for elderly persons. The unique needs of the elderly in disaster contexts obviously warrant special consideration in the delivery of post-disaster relief, but those needs were not hypothesized to have required or resulted in a greater average number of referrals in encounters when compared to other age groups. It was, however, hypothesized they would receive less referrals and data indicate this did not happen. Findings suggest social vulnerability for elderly participants was therefore not magnified, but they cannot, however, also say that vulnerability among the elderly was potentially mitigated by MPR referrals.

Sex, on the other hand, was hypothesized to show statistically significant group differences and effects on referrals. Although previous research states that women demonstrate greater social vulnerability in disaster, it was hypothesized they would receive a higher average number of referrals when compared to men due to presumed greater socio-emotional and expressive skills. With more referrals at their disposal, women might be better linked to recovery resources, thereby reducing their overall vulnerability. Results suggest referrals were distributed equitably between women and men. However, further analyses using two-way ANOVA tests to compare women across racial/ethnic groups might reveal significant referrals means differences between minority and White women. Interaction effects between race/ethnicity and sex could also therefore be controlled. Moreover, if a reliable and accurate measure of parental status was available, results could be interpreted more meaningfully for whether or not equal distribution among sexes, within or between racial/ethnic groups, could actually signify equitable distribution given childcare responsibilities. Without more detailed knowledge of family contexts, conclusions about *sex* remain limited.

Findings of difference by *race/ethnicity* affirmed hypotheses of difference, but in unexpected ways. The Asian sample was not anticipated to show higher mean referrals when compared to other groups. Results defied expectations that White participants would demonstrate the highest *total* and *instrumental referrals* means and that Black participants would show higher means for all referrals when compared to Asian participants. Analyses appear to dispel original hypotheses that differences would disadvantage socially vulnerable groups and reflect a practice of biased relief delivery.

However, findings must be considered within data and analytical limitations. No statistically significant differences in referrals means between White, Black, and Latino participants cannot be presumed to reflect relatively equal need and/or equal resources available. Although referrals were technically distributed equitably between White, Black, and Latino participants, the value of those referrals are likely to vary dramatically if individual SES and possessed resources were able to be considered. Data findings might, therefore, nonetheless mask biased and discriminatory effects of seemingly equitable referrals distribution. In addition, biases might nonetheless have still affected referrals distribution, but outliers on either side could have had an equalizing effect for group outcomes.

However, although it cannot be determined from data whether or not Asian participants actually demonstrated greater need for referrals when compared to other groups, the advantage demonstrated among the Asian sample is believed to have resulted in largest part due to commonalities in language and culture shared between participants and MPR staff.

Data reveal that 52% of Asian participants preferred another language and that the majority of these "other" languages preferred were Vietnamese and Thai, which reflect the ethnic make-up of the local Asian population. Of this percentage that preferred another language of contact, 38% actually participated in an interview using that preferred language. This means that linguistic and cultural barriers were eliminated for 73% of the Asian participants who might have otherwise had difficulty communicating needs in English to a potentially non-Thai or Vietnamese speaking relief worker. When compared to Latino participants who preferred Spanish, the same percentage (52%) preferred Spanish, but only 19% were actually interviewed in Spanish. Linguistic barriers were therefore only eliminated for 37% of Latino participants. Moreover, of that 37%, it cannot be assumed that encounters yielded the same level of cultural identification as is presumed within the Asian sample.

Given the broader array of non-Latino individuals now able to speak Spanish, it cannot be assumed that encounters that occurred in Spanish were necessarily conducted by a relief worker of Latino descent. Encounters in Vietnamese and Thai, however, might be assumed to have been conducted by relief workers of Vietnamese and Thai descent given the lesser prevalence of those languages when compared to Spanish. By linguistic necessity then, the Asian sample is believed to have required that interviewee-interviewer scenarios be matched by culture and ethnicity. Even if Latino participants were also matched with interviewers by ethnicity, MPR does not seem to have accommodated the language needs of Latino participants as well when compared to Asian participants.

However, it is believed that in encounters where participants were matched with MPR outreach staff by ethnicity and culture, an interpersonal social space was created where biases and cultural prejudices and/or institutional mistrust that might have otherwise been present in other scenarios, were mostly absent. This dynamic is believed to have enabled cultural identification between the interviewer and interviewee, which encouraged more self disclosure and communication of need on the part of the participant. The effect was that needs were more effectively identified and better able to be addressed by the MPR staff worker, by way of referrals. As a result, Asian participants have overall higher referrals means when compared to Spanish-only speaking Latino participants, whose language needs were less successfully met., and when compared to White and Black participants, whose interviewers' language and demographic backgrounds cannot be identified.

However, although no information on MPR staff member demographics is available, photos from the MPR final report show a seemingly diverse staff by race/ethnicity, gender, and age. Service delivery, as a former MPR worker indicated (personal interview with Kirkland 2006), was often designed with cultural sensitivity in mind and staff members of particular racial/ethnic groups were frequently deployed where members of their groups most frequently resided, particularly for zip codes with higher minority populations. This strategy might explain the data's seeming lack of visible bias against racial/ethnic minorities. Furthermore, this strategy might also explain why statistically significant, positive effects were found between expressive referrals and the % Black within the Black sample, if Black staff members were directed to those zip codes with higher percentages of Black residents. However, there is no question that Asian staff members able to speak Vietnamese and Thai had to be deployed in the zip codes of Biloxi where Asian participants resided in greatest number.

In sum, findings suggest that Mississippi Project Recovery successfully delivered more equitable assistance so as to not magnify pre-existing social vulnerability among affected MS Gulf Coast residents, and seemingly defied the pattern of discriminatory relief delivery found in previous disaster research. However, further two-way ANOVA comparisons of means and/or stepwise multivariate regression analyses that limit interaction effects, particularly between *sex* and *race/ethnicity*, might reveal biases that are currently undetected with the chosen analyses. Moreover, if more was known about individual-level SES, the resources available to participants at the time of referrals, and how referrals given relate to demonstrated needs, seemingly equitable referrals distribution could be revealed to have not been particularly helpful to participants when personal circumstances are considered. As a result, findings must be considered in the context of these serious data limitations and conclusions remain somewhat superficial.

Conclusion

Disasters not only allow us to more clearly locate the fault lines of social vulnerability, they also provide a unique opportunity to study how the distribution of recovery resources is channeled along those lines and reproduces structures of inequality. However, it should not be assumed this process happens in a supra-human realm beyond the control of individual agents. Human beings, although often unaware of our roles in the processes that create and maintain macro-level structural inequality, are not limited to passive acceptance of the social structures and historical conditions we inherit and must exercise conscious agency in thought and behavior that might otherwise perform subconsciously. Mississippi Project Recovery data suggest that the reproduction of inequality is not a fixed outcome in post-disaster resource mobilization. Referrals data suggest MPR equitably distributed referrals to instrumental and expressive resources in crisis counseling encounters with Katrina victims living on the Mississippi Gulf Coast. If referrals functioned in the way they were intended, then MPR potentially opened access to resources that might have otherwise been unknown or out of reach among traditionally vulnerable groups.

Although it cannot be concluded with certainty what specific factors enabled MPR referrals to be distributed seemingly equitably, it is believed that strategically identifying and targeting socially vulnerable groups and communities is partially responsible for successful outcomes. This enabled MPR to extend its reach to traditionally underserved groups and communities and also suggests a critical awareness of vulnerability as a phenomenon influencing disaster impact and recovery. Another benefit likely came from employing local residents with local knowledge of where these vulnerable groups and communities could be found. Particularly given the size and heterogeneity of some coastal cities of Mississippi, service delivery might have been less effective without knowledge of local social demographics.

However, because this study specifically measured the referrals outcomes demonstrated from one-on-one interviews, which means data already represent who was reached, equitable distribution of referrals among participants suggest evidence of a critical awareness translated to service practice. This was likely to have been fostered in the training MPR employees received, although more information, perhaps best collected through qualitative interviews in a follow-up study with former MPR employees, is needed to make this determination. This was also likely to have been encouraged by the cultural competencies employed by staff members. As stated previously, no employee demographic data is available, but photos of employee teams indicate a diverse staff by race, ethnicity, sex, and age. If, as was indicated by a former MPR staff member (Personal Interview with Kirkland 2006), outreach workers were trained in culturally-sensitive delivery and counseling methods, one would expect findings might indicate this knowledge was successfully implemented in encounters. Again, utilizing local residents able to also exercise cultural competencies specific to the Mississippi Gulf Coast area is believed to have further facilitated success in encounters. Presumptions are supported by findings from the Asian sample, whose referrals means were highest, that indicate a large portion of its participants engaged in encounters with MPR staff from similar, if not the same, cultural and/or linguistic background.

However, the effects of MPR referrals distribution in mitigating social vulnerability can only be postulated within the rather significant data limitations. Considering that no income, damage, or follow-up data for individual participants is known, caution must be exercised in data interpretation. Nothing is known about the resources that were already available to MPR participants, the specific needs demonstrated by participants and whether or not referrals received represented a good match, or whether or not participants actually used referrals and received resources. Moreover, although findings suggest MPR did not contribute to a reproduction of social inequality by means of biased referrals distribution against socially vulnerable groups, they obviously cannot and do not negate the presence and effects of countless other formats where social inequality could have been reproduced in Katrina recovery on the Mississippi Gulf Coast. Results are also not meant to suggest that MPR staff members were completely without bias as a result of their training or presumed cultural competencies. Biases could have still nonetheless manifested in encounters conducted by staff members professionally trained in culturally sensitive counseling methods. If interviews had been recorded, conversation analyses could be conducted to further examine this topic. However, because they were not, available data are the only window for viewing whether or not biases intervened in encounters to reproduce group inequalities and social vulnerability.

The case of Hurricane Katrina brought to light the consequences deeply entrenched social inequities hold for disaster. Popular assumptions viewed recovery from Katrina as an opportunity to reverse the historical consequences of social inequality and discrimination. However, as previous disaster research shows, power structures are highly resistant to change and tend to be reproduced in disaster through disparities in access to resources. If the goals of CCPs are to link affected individuals to resources needed for recovery, in order to do so equitably, the individuals and organizations creating those links must be sensitive to the phenomena of social vulnerability in their relations with and delivery of care to disaster victims. In effect, the potential exists to avoid further exacerbation of the reproduction of social inequality after disaster.

About the Author

Kelli is a native of Pascagoula, MS and worked and collected information on recovery efforts along the Mississippi Gulf Coast following Katrina. Her presentation provided a specific example of one post-Katrina mental health care program delivered in an impact area that has gained little publicity. She completed her M.A. from the Department of Sociology at the University of Wyoming in 2009. She worked for the Gulf Coast Fair Housing Center in Gulfport, MS. Her areas of research included race, class, gender, social vulnerability and natural disasters, disaster mental health, and cross-cultural trauma. Kelli presented the final results of her research and work at the Rocky Mountain Disaster Mental Health Conference held in Cheyenne, Wyoming in November 2009.

References

Aptekar, Lewis. 1994. *Environmental Disasters in Global Perspective*. Toronto, ON: G. K. Hall and Co.

Benight, Charles C. and Albert Bandura. 2004. "Social Cognitive Theory of Posttraumatic Recovery: The Role of Perceived Self-Efficacy." *Behaviour Research and Therapy* 42: 1129-148.

Bonilla-Silva, Eduardo. 2003. *Racism Without Racists: Color-Blind Racism and the Persistence of Racial Inequality in the United States*. Lanham, MD: Rowman & Littlefield Publishers, Inc.

Bolin, Robert. C. and Lois Stanford. 1998. *The Northridge Earthquake: Vulnerability and Disaster*. London: Routledge.

Bourque, Linda B., Judith M. Siegel, Megumi Kano and Michele M. Wood. 2006. "Shelter from the Storm: Repairing the National Emergency Management System After Hurricane Katrina." *The Annals of the American Academy of Political and Social Science* 604:129-48.

Crabbs, Michael A. and Edward Heffron. 1981. "Loss Associated with a Natural Disaster." *The Personnel and Guidance Journal* 59: 378-82.

Cutter, Susan L. and Christopher T. Emerich. 2006. "Moral Hazard, Social Catastrophe: The Changing Face of Vulnerability along the Hurricane Coasts." *The Annals of the American Academy of Political and Social Science* 604:102-12

Cutter, Susan L., Bryan J. Boruff and W. Lynn Shirley. 2003. "Social Vulnerability to Environmental Hazards." *Social Science Quarterly*. 84:242-61.

Dynes, Russell. R. 1970. *Organized Behavior in Disaster*. Lexington, MA: Heath Lexington Books.

Dyson, Michael Eric. 2006. *Come Hell or High Water: Hurricane Katrina and the Color of Disaster*. New York, NY: Basic Civitas.

Edwards, Margie L. Kiter. 1998. "An Interdisciplinary Perspective on Disaster and Stress: The Promise of an Ecological Framework." *Sociological Forum* 13:115-32.

Elliot, James R. and Jeremy Pais. 2006. "Race, Class, and Hurricane Katrina: Social Differences in Human Responses to Disaster." *Social Science Research* 35:295-321.

Enarson, Elaine. 2006. "Women and Girls Last? Averting the Second Post Katrina Disaster." *Understanding Katrina: Perspectives from the Social Sciences, Social Science Research Center*. Retrieved October 8, 2006 http://understandingkatrina.ssrc.org/Enarson/pf/.

Enarson, Elaine and Betty Hearn Morrow. 1997. "A Gendered Perspective: The Voices of Women." Pp. 116-41 in *Hurricane Andrew: Ethnicity, Gender, and the Sociology of Disasters*, edited by Walter Gillis Peacock, Betty Hearn Morrow and Hugh Gladwin. New York, NY: Routledge.

Erickson, Kai T. 1976. *Everything in Its Path: Destruction of Community in the Buffalo Creek Flood*. New York, NY: Simon and Schuster.

Feagin, Joe R. and Clairece Booher Feagin. 2007. "Theoretical Perspectives in Race and Ethnic Relations." Pp. 29-45 in *Rethinking the Color Line: Readings in Race and Ethnicity*, 3rd ed., edited by Charles A Gallagher. Boston, MA: McGraw-Hill.

Flint, Courtney G. and A. E. Luloff. 2005. "Natural Resource-Based Communities, Risk, and Disaster: An Intersection of Theories." *Society and Natural Resources* 18:399-412.

Fothergill, Alice. 1996. "The Neglect of Gender in Disaster Work: An Overview of the Literature." *International Journal of Mass Emergencies and Disasters* 14:33-56.

Fothergill, Alice, Enrique G.M. Maestas, and JoAnne DeRouen Darlington. 1999. "Race, Ethnicity and Disasters in the United States: A Review of the Literature." *Disasters* 23: 156-173.

Galambos, Colleen M. 2005. "Natural Disasters: Health and Mental Health Considerations." *Health and Social Work* 30:83-86.

García-Acosta, Virginia. 2002. "Historical Disaster Research." Pp. 49-66 in *Catastrophe and Culture: The Anthropology of Disaster*, edited by Susanna M. Hoffman and Anthony Oliver-Smith. Santa Fe, NM: School of American Research Press.

Garrett, Thomas A. and Russel S. Sobel. 2003. "The Political Economy of FEMA Disaster Payments." *Economic Inquiry* 41:496-509.

Garrison, Carol Z., Elizabeth S. Bryant, Cheryll Addy, Pamela G. Spurrier, John R. Freedy, and Dean G. Kilpatrick. 1995. "Posttraumatic Stress Disorder in Adolescents after Hurricane Andrew." *Journal of the American Academy of Child and Adolescent Psychiatry* 34:1193-99.

Gittleman, Martin. 2004. "Disasters and Psychosocial Rehabilitation." *International Journal of Mental Health* 32:51-69.

Gladwin, Hugh and Walter Gillis Peacock. 1997. "Warning and Evacuation: A Night for Hard Houes." Pp. 52-75 in *Hurricane Andrew: Ethnicity, Gender, and the Sociology of Disasters*, edited by Walter

Gillis Peacock, Betty Hearn Morrow and Hugh Gladwin. New York, NY: Routledge.

Green, Bonnie L., Jacob D. Lindy, and Mary C. Grace. 1990. "Buffalo Creek Survivors in the Second Decade: Stability of Stress Symptoms." *American Journal of Orthopsychiatry* 60:43-54.

Haas, J. Eugene, Robert W. Kates, and Martyn J. Bowden. 1977. *Reconstruction Following Disaster*. Cambridge, MA: The MIT Press.

Hartmand, Chester and Gregory D. Squires. 2006. *There Is No Such Thing as a Natural Disaster: Race, Class, and Hurricane Katrina*. New York, NY: Taylor and Francis Group.

Hazards and Vulnerability Research Institute. 2006. "Social Vulnerability Index for the United States." Columbia, SC: Hazards and Vulnerability Research Institute. Retrieved February 12, 2007 http://www.cas.sc.edu/geog/hrl/sovi.html.

Healey, Joseph F. 1998. *Race, Ethnicity, Gender, and Class*. 2nd ed. Thousand Oaks, CA: Pine Forge Press.

Hobfoll, Stevan E. 1988. *The Ecology of Stress*. New York, NY: Hemisphere Publishing Corporation.

Hobfoll, Stevan E. 1998. *Stress, Culture, and Community: The Psychology and Philosophy of Stress*. New York, NY: Plenum Press.

Hurst, Charles E. 2007. *Social Inequality: Forms, Causes, and Consequences*. 6th ed. Boston, MA: Pearson Education, Inc.

Jackson, James S. and Katherine M. Knight. 2006. "Race and Self Regulatory Health Behaviors: The Role of the Stress Response and the HPA Axis in Physical and Mental Health Disparities." Pp. 189-207 in *Social Structures, Aging, and Self Regulation in the Elderly*, edited by K. Warner Schaie and Laura Carstensen. New York, NY: Springer Publishing Company.

Jackson, James S. and Marita R. Inglehart. 1995. "Reverberation Theory: Stress and Racism in Hierarchically Structured Communities." Pp. 353-73 in *Extreme Stress and Communities: Impact and Intervention*, edited by S. E. Hobfoll and M.W. deVries, New York, NY: Springer Publishing Company.

Jones-DeWeever, Avis A. and Heidi Hartmann. 2006. "Abandoned Before the Storms: The Glaring Disaster of Gender, Race, and Class Disparities in the Gulf." Pp. 85-101 in *There Is No Such Thing as a Natural Disaster: Race, Class, and Hurricane Katrina* edited by Chester Hartman and Gregory D. Squires. New York, NY: Routledge.

Kamel, Nabil M.O. and Anastasia Loukaitou-Sideris. 2004. "Residential Assistance and Recovery Following the Northridge Earthquake." *Urban Studies* 41:533-62.

Kaniasty, Kryzsztof and Fran H. Norris. 2000. "Help-Seeking Comfort and Receiving Social Support: The Role of Ethnicity and Context of Need." *American Journal of Community Psychology* 28:545-81.

Kessler, Ronald, Sandro Galea, Russell T. Jones, and Holly A. Parker. 2006. "Mental Illness and Suicidality after Hurricane Katrina." *Bulletin of the World Health Organization* 84:12. Retrieved February 16, 2006 http://www.who.int/bulletin/volumes/84/12/06-033019.pdf.

Kleiner, Anna M., John J. Green and Albert B. Nylander III. 2007. "A Community Study of Disaster Impacts and Redevelopment Issues Facing East Biloxi, Mississippi" in *The sociology of Katrina: Perspectives on a modern catastrophe*. Edited by David L. Brunsma, David Overfelt, and J. Steven Picou. Rowan & Littlefield Publishers, Lanham, MD.

Kreps, G. A. 1984. "Sociological Inquiry and Disaster Research." *Annual Review of Sociology* 10:309-30.

Lima, Bruno R. and Martin Gittelman. 2004. "Differential and Long-Term Effects of Disasters: The Need for Planning and Preparation (Editor's Introduction). *International Journal of Mental Health* 43:3-5.

Litz, Brett T., Matt J. Gray, Richard A. Bryant, and Amy B. Adler. 2002. "Early Intervention for Trauma: Current Status and Future Directions." *Clinical Psychology: Science and Practice* 9:112-34.

Lott, Bernice. 2007. "Psychology, Social Class, and Resources for Human Welfare." Pp. 47-76 in *Psychology and Economic Injustice: Personal, Professional and Political Intersections (Psychology of Women)* by Bernice E. Lott and Heather E. Bullock. Washington, D.C.: American Psychological Association.

Lyndsey, Linda L. 1997. *Gender Roles: A Sociological Perspective*. 3rd ed. Upper Saddle River, NJ: Prentice-Hall, Inc.

May, Peter J. 1985. *Recovering from Catastrophes: Federal Disaster Relief Policies and Politics*. Westport, CT: Greenwood Press.

Marger, Martin N. 1999. *Social Inequality: Patterns and Processes*. Mountain View, CA: Mayfield Publishing Company.

Massey, Douglas S. and Nancy A. Denton. 1993. "American Apartheid: The Perpetuation of the Underclass." Pp. 316-336 in *Rethinking the Color Line: Readings in Race and Ethnicity* by Charles A. Gallagher. Boston, MA: McGraw-Hill.

Merton, Robert K. 1968. "The Matthew effect in science." *Science* 159: 56-63. Morrow, Betty Hearn. 1999. "Identifying and Mapping Community Vulnerability." *Disasters* 23:1-18.

Murphy, Shirley A. 1985. "The Conceptual Bases for Disaster Research and Intervention." Pp. 3-21 in *Perspectives on Disaster Recovery* edited by Jerri Laube and Shirley A. Murphy. Norwalk, CT: Appleton Century-Crofts.

The National Center for PTSD. 2006. *Evaluating and Monitoring the Reach, Quality, and Consistency of Crisis Counseling Programs: Manual and Toolkit*. White River Junction, VT: The National Center for PTSD, Department of Veterans Affairs.

Norris, Fran H., Matthew J. Friedman, Patricia J. Watson, Christopher M. Byrne, Eolia Diaz, and Krzysztof Kaniasty. 2002. "60,000 Disaster Victims Speak: Part I. An Empirical Review of the Empirical Literature, 1981-2001." *Psychiatry* 65:240-60.

Oliver-Smith, Anthony A. 2002. "Theorizing Disasters: Nature, Power, and Culture." Pp. 23-47 in *Catastrophe and Culture: The Anthropology of Disaster*, edited by Susanna M. Hoffman and Anthony Oliver-Smith. Santa Fe, NM: School of American Research Press.

Oliver-Smith, Anthony and Susan M. Hoffman. 2002. "Why Anthropologists Should Study Disasters." Pp. 3-22 in *Catastrophe and Culture: The Anthropology of Disaster*, edited by Susanna M. Hoffman and Anthony Oliver-Smith. Santa Fe, NM: School of American Research Press.

Palm, Risa I. 1990. *Natural Hazards: An Integrative Framework for Research and Planning*. Baltimore, MD: The Johns Hopkins University Press.

Park, Yoosun and Joshua Miller. 2006. "The Social Ecology of Hurricane Katrina: Re-Writing the Discourse of 'Natural' Disasters." *Smith College Studies in Social Work* 76:9-24.

Pavkov, Thomas W., Dan A. Lewis, and John S. Lyons. 1989. "Psychiatric Diagnoses and Racial Bias: An Empirical Investigation."*Professional Psychology: Research and Practice* 20(6): 364-368.

Peacock, Walter and Chris Girard. 1997. "Ethic and Racial Inequalities in Hurricane Damage and Insurance Settlements. Pp. 171-191 in *Hurricane Andrew: Ethnicity, Gender, and the Sociology of Disasters*, edited by Walter Gillis Peacock, Betty Hearn Morrow and Hugh Gladwin. New York, NY: Routledge.

Peacock, Walter Gillis and A. Kathleen Ragsdale. 1997. "Social Systems, Ecological Networks and Disasters: Toward a Socio-Political Ecology of Disasters." Pp. 20-34 in *Hurricane Andrew: Ethnicity, Gender, and the Sociology of Disasters*, edited by Walter Gillis Peacock, Betty Hearn Morrow and Hugh Gladwin. New York, NY: Routledge.

Pellow, David Naguib and Robert J. Brulle. 2005. "Power, Justice, and the Environment: Toward Critical Environmental Justice Studies." Pp. 1-19 in *Power, Justice, and the Environment*, edited by David Naguib Pellow and Robert J. Brulle. Cambridge, MA: The MIT Press.

Perilla, Julia L., Fran H. Norris, and Evelyn A. Lavizzo. 2002. "Ethnicity, Culture, and Disaster Response: Identifying and Explaining Ethnic Differences in PTSD Six Months after Hurricane Andrew." *Journal of Social and Clinical Psychology*. 21:20-45.

Personal interview with Alexis Kirkland, April 5, 2007. Powell, John A., Hasan Kwame Jeffries, Daniel W. Newhart, and Eric Stiens. 2006. "Towards a Transformative View of Race: The Crisis and Opportunity of Katrina." Pp. 59-84 in *There Is No Such Thing as a Natural Disaster: Race, Class, and Hurricane Katrina*, edited by Chester Hartman and Gregory D. Squires. New York, NY: Routledge.

Quarantelli, E. L. and Russel R. Dynes. 1976. "Community Conflict: Its Absence and Its Presence in Natural Disasters. *Mass Emergencies* 1:139-52. Reilly, Benjamin. 2009. *Disaster and Human History: Case Studies in Nature, Society and Catastrophe*. Jefferson, NC: McFarland & Company, Inc.

Shaw, Rosalind. 1989. "Living with floods in Bangladesh." *Anthropology Today* 5:11-13.

Smith, Bruce W. and John R. Freedy. 2000. "Psychosocial Resource Loss as a Mediator of the Effects of Flood Exposure on Psychological Distress and Physical Symptoms." *Journal of Traumatic Stress* 13:349-57.

Spence, Patrick R., Kenneth A. Lachlan, and Donyale R. Griffin. 2007. "Crisis Communication, Race, and Natural Disasters." *Journal of Black Studies* 37:539-54. Spiegel, Alix. 2007. "Hurricane Katrina's Mental Health Worsens."

National Public Radio. Retrieved November 1, 2007 http://www.npr.org/templates/story/story.php?storyId=15835042.

Stallings, Robert A. 2002. "Weberian Political Sociology and Sociological Disaster Studies." *Sociological Forum* 17:281-305.

Tierney, Kathleen J. 2007. "From the margins to the mainstream? Disaster research at a crossroads." *Annual Review of Sociology* 33: 503-25.

Tierney, Kathleen J. Michael K. Lindell, and Ronald W. Perry. 2001.*Facing the Unexpected: Disaster Preparedness in the United States*. Washington, D.C.: Joseph Henry Press.

United States Department of Commerce 2006. *Service assessment: Hurricane Katrina, August 23-31, 2005*. Silver Spring, MD: National Oceanic and Atmospheric Administration and National Weather Service.

Ursano, Robert J., Frederick P. Cerise, Robert DeMartino, Dorris B. Reissman, and Mary Katherine Shear. 2006. "The Impact of Disasters and their Aftermath on Mental Health." *Journal of Clinical Psychiatry* 67:7-14.

Voelker, R. 2006. "Post-Katrina Mental Health Needs Prompt Group to Compile Disaster Medicine Guide." *Journal of the American Medical Association*. January 18, 295:259-60.

Wang, Philip S., Michael J. Gruber, Richard E. Powers, Michael Schoenbaum, Anthony H. Speier, Kenneth B. Wells, and Ronald C. Kessler. 2007. "Mental Health Service Use Among Hurricane Katrina Survivors in the Eight Months After the Disaster." *Psychiatric Services* 58:1403-11.

Including People With Functional and Access Needs in All Aspects of Community Disaster Planning

David Schaad, MHR, NREMT-B,

Coordinator, Community Services
Wyoming Institute for Disabilities (WIND),
College of Health Sciences, University of Wyoming.

It doesn't take much foresight, forethought or imagination to realize people with mobility, vision, cognitive or other impairments have extra challenges getting out of harm's way. We need only consider images, facts and figures from large scale worldwide disasters of recent years in order to validate people with disabilities will likely be on the "short end of the stick" unless specific targeted planning efforts within communities mitigate their personal harm.

Wyoming Institute for Disabilities (WIND) has been the lead agency in working with the Wyoming Office of Homeland Security (WOHS), the Wyoming Department of Health (WDH) and county Homeland Security/Emergency Management Coordinators (EMAs or HSCs). Conference participants gained information about past and present efforts in working with emergency planners and reviewed resources in support of personal planning for people with disabilities and other people with access and functional needs. A primary focus of UTSE is to be a local resource for county Homeland Security/Emergency Management Coordinators, EMS, Fire, Law Enforcement, Public Health, Hospital Preparedness staff and others involved in local emergency management planning.

WIND is a UCEDD (University Center for Excellence in Developmental Disabilities) housed within the College of Health Sciences at the University of Wyoming and is one of sixty-seven such entities nationwide. The UCEDD mission serves people with disabilities through research, education and community services on university campuses and medical schools throughout the United States. For more information about University Centers for Excellence in Developmental Disabilities, see the website www.aucd.org.

Participants received paper and electronic versions of reference articles, targeted handouts and other relevant materials. Wyoming focus is on individual responsibility and choice based upon accurate first-hand information. Many people with disabilities simply have not considered preparation for emergencies as a personal responsibility while others with much to offer, have not formally connected with disaster response organizations. WIND efforts seek to bridge that gap. WIND's focus is consistent with the theme of the conference in terms of helping move people with disabilities from victims requiring rescue to rescue planners and full community participants. Planning efforts result in increased community awareness and inclusive preparation for all types of emergencies and hazards.

Everyone is aware of the impact of the Twin Towers and Hurricanes Ivan and Katrina events on people who could not run from harm's way. Following these events, the US Department of Health and Human Services and the US Office of Homeland Security held a joint conference to address issues relevant to people with disabilities in an attempt to encourage local planning to reduce and/or mitigate the negative effects of large-scale disasters on people with disabilities.

The challenges facing emergency planners and responders when planning for needs of fragments of their service population are not unlike the typical human service challenges for serving fragments of their service population. Within the community, both individuals and their needs differ. The handy "one-size fits all" approach clearly does not cover the needs of everyone. Emergency planners and responders cannot go to one group or one agency—either at state or local level—and readily identify people who might need help in an emergency. Hence the need for large scale outreach efforts.

Wyoming's focus to include people with disabilities in disaster planning includes all people who cannot run from harm's way. Wyoming created an acronym for people in this category and to more simply educate the first response community about planning for and helping people who may need help in emergencies. This effort is centered on the acronym "UTSE" for people Unable To Self Evacuate.

Included in the population of emergency response personnel, are people who provide services and supports in communities to people with disabilities and others who might need help in emergencies. Appendix 1 is a living document which lists likely categories of people UTSE. One need only read over the list to consider the potential magnitude of loss in a large scale disaster. Fortunately for Wyoming planners, we are not faced with populations the size of New York City, San Francisco, New Orleans or sites of other major disasters. Nonetheless, emergency planners bear the same level of responsibility for including all populations of people in emergency planning.

Appendix 3 identifies the top 10 major disasters in US history. Excerpts are provided which provide clues to populations of some of the people Wyoming would consider as members of the UTSE population, according to Appendix 1. As might be expected, people in the category of UTSE are more susceptible to death and injury than populations of people who can run from harm's way.

Wyoming developed an initiative around UTSE with several objectives. The primary objective is to bring together emergency planners in communities, with consumers (people who may need help in emergencies) and with service and support agencies who serve populations of people UTSE. WIND conducts ongoing community workshops in communities which centers on that objective.

Another objective is to increase personal readiness of people with disabilities and others with access and functional needs. WIND emphasizes two types of readiness; short term and long term. Short term efforts focus mostly on emergency evacuation and being ready while longer term efforts focus mostly on evacuation preparation for periods of days and weeks. A plethora of information about personal readiness exists on a number of websites. One need only "Google" "emergency preparedness for people with disabilities."

The needs of people UTSE are the same as the needs of other people but for a variety of reasons, accessibility of information in easy-to-understand and alternative formats, is not abundant. People UTSE are often among the most vulnerable in communities. I use the illustration of TSA airport guards, particularly during period of upgraded alerts. I often ask people, "As an airline passenger, how much control do you have over TSA security guards and what they do?" Obviously, the answer ranges between little and none. Many people in the UTSE category (again, look over the Appendix 1 list) have little to no control or direct access in communities to agencies and entities with responsibility for emergency planning and/or response.

A core advisory group was formed to help guide Wyoming's efforts. The UTSE Core Advisory Group or UTSE CAG, developed the following vision, mission statement and goals to help guide statewide efforts:

Vision: We envision full inclusion of people Unable To Self Evacuate, into community emergency response planning and exercises within each Wyoming county.

Mission Statement: Provide information and technical support to assist communities in all-hazards planning and exercises, in cooperation with and an emphasis on people UTSE; and facilitate planning between consumers, disabilities entities and emergency preparedness and response personnel.

Goals:

- Inclusion of people UTSE in disaster planning and scenarios in all counties
- All people with disabilities in Wyoming will have personal and personal emergency plans
- All counties will have fully accessible shelters for people UTSE
- All counties will have provisions (DME and service animals) to support requirements of ADA Chapter 7
- All hospitals will have plans and procedures established to meet the needs of people UTSE

The UTSE CAG consists mostly of people with a variety of impairments which would likely necessitate assistance in an emergency. The UTSE CAG identified the following list of entities as major community partners, with acknowledgement of the need to include entities for senior citizens and planning for mothers with children who have special needs:

- Citizens with disabilities and other people who may need help during emergencies
- Emergency Management and first on-scene agency representatives
- Hospitals
- Public health representatives
- Disability organization representatives
- Volunteer organizations
- Mental Health Providers

Mental health providers can especially help in planning and in disasters by underwriting the concepts of inclusion and accessibility in all their emergency thoughts and plans. Many mental health center clients are people with forms of intellectual and/or developmental impairment. Mental health providers can look at the array of behavioral manifestations of diagnoses and disability and help educate first response personnel about behaviors which can easily be misperceived as uncooperativeness, non-compliance and disobedience.

Mental health practitioners can also provide useful information to emergency planners and community health professionals about medications and medication management especially regarding stockpiles for people with behavioral medication prescriptions. Law enforcement will have enough to contend with without having to focus on people with mental or behavioral health challenges.

About the Author

W. David Schaad, MHR, NREMT-B, is the Coordinator for Community Services at the Wyoming Institute for Disabilities (WIND), University of Wyoming. WIND is Wyoming's University Centers for Excellence in Developmental Disabilities (UCEDD). You may contact him at dschaad@uwyo.edu or call 307.766.2095.

Appendix 1: Identifying People Unable To Self-Evacuate (UTSE)

Schools

- K-12 schools (public and private)

At-Large in Neighborhoods

- Mothers and Children with Special Health Care Needs
- Elderly
- People With Disabilities

Community Facilities

- Mental Health Centers (public and private)
- Wyoming State Hospital
- Wyoming Life Resource Center
- Veterans Hospitals and Centers
- Independent Living Centers
- Group Homes
- Residential Treatment Programs
- Hospitals and Clinics
- Nursing Homes/Residential Facilities for senior citizens
- Residential Facilities for people with disabilities
- Senior/Daytime Activity Centers
- Hospice Centers
- Day care centers
- Other-state resources to house people with disabilities and other vulnerable populations
- Day Habilitation Centers (vocational rehabilitation)
- Resorts and Hotels

Court Related

- Prisons
- Jails
- Honor Farm
- Wyoming Boys School
- Wyoming Girls School

Government Partners

- Mayors/Town Managers
- Wyoming Association for Municipalities
- Military Installations

- Veteran's Administrations Properties
- Wind River Reservation
- Border State Resources
- Private Business
- Employers

Appendix 2: Ten Deadliest American Natural Disasters

Galveston, Texas Hurricane (September 18, 1900)

More than 6,000 men, women and children lost their lives during the Great Storm. Among the dead were 10 sisters and 90 children from the St. Mary's Orphans Asylum. The hurricane hit the Caribbean, then moved onward and upward to Florida's Atlantic coast. From Fort Pierce to Palm Beach, buildings shattered and splintered as the big wind blew, but its final fury was spent on the tiny farming communities that dot Lake Okeechobee's southern shore. In roughly six hours—no one knows exactly how long—winds churned the water in that shallow lake, the humble muck dike broke and a wall of water spilled out of the lake with the destructive force of a tidal wave. In a matter of hours, towns from Clewiston to Canal Point—home to 6,000 people—were awash in a sea of disaster. Reference http://www.1900storm.com/orphanage.lasso

Great Okeechobee Hurricane, Florida (September 16-17, 1928)

Coastal residents living along Palm Beach, Florida, were basically prepared for this category 4 hurricane, but it was along the south shores of Lake Okeechobee in the Florida Everglades that most of the 2000+ victims perished. Many were migrant workers working in such an isolated location, that they had no warning of the impending disaster. Over 1,000 bodies were burned due to decomposition and impending biohazards because burial details could not keep up with the job.
http://www.sun-sentinel.com/news/weather/hurricane/sfl-1928-hurricane,0,2734526.story

Johnstown, PA Flood (May 31, 1889)

May 31st marks the anniversary of the Johnstown Flood, one of the worst disasters in American history. It was on this day in 1889 near the town of Johnstown, Pennsylvania, that the South Fork Dam collapsed, sending a massive wall of water down river that killed more than 2,000 people. In 1964, the Johnstown Flood National Memorial was authorized as a unit of the National Park Service. The 165-acre memorial tells the story of the fateful event in southwestern Pennsylvania. As part of the annual commemoration, more than 2,209 candles are lit as a way of remembering those who died in the Flood. The official death toll registered 2,209 people killed or presumed lost. Among the dead were 99 entire families, 396 children under the age of 10, and 777 unidentified victims. There were 1,600 homes lost, 280 businesses destroyed, and $17 million in property damage as a result of the Flood.
http://usparks.about.com/cs/parkhistory/a/johnstownflood.htm

Chenier Caminada Hurricane (October 1, 1893)

In the late nineteenth century, the French-speaking but multi-ethnic community of about 1700 persons served as the major supplier of fish and shellfish to the restaurants of New Orleans. On the night of Sunday, October 1st, 1893, the history, economy, settlement, and ancestry of Cheniere Caminada and all of Southeastern Louisiana was forcibly changed forever. Originating near the Yucatan Peninsula, a compact and fast-moving hurricane rode a low pressure trough across the river and bayou plains of extreme Southeastern Louisiana at such an angle that the wall of Gulf waters it drove traversed the peninsula of Cheniere Caminada three times. Before exiting the continent from North Carolina some ten days later, it had killed nearly 2000 persons, the vast majority from coastal Southeastern Louisiana. On

Cheniere Caminada alone, it killed nearly 900, including half the women and nearly all the children.

Reference: http://www.1893hurricane.com/

"Sea Islands" Hurricane (August 27-28, 1893)

It is estimated that the "Great Storm of 1893" that struck the southern South Carolina and northern Georgia coast was at least a Category 4 storm, but there is no way of knowing, since measures of hurricane intensity weren't measured for storms before 1900. The storm killed an estimated 1,000 - 2,000 people, mostly from storm surge affecting the low-lying barrier "Sea Islands" off the Carolina coast. One peculiarity of this storm was that the aged, the very young, and the infirm were all killed. The survivors were young men in the vigor of manhood. Very few were seriously wounded, and hundreds were found without a bruise on their bodies. They were killed by the sheer pressure and fury of the wind. In the settlements where the storm was worst, not a single child survived, and very few women. At *Cheniere Caminada*, opposite Grand Island, 822 people perished. Of these 496 were children. From this one settlement 240 fishermen were lost at sea in their boats—more than one thousand dead out of a community of 1,640 souls. There were 310 houses in the settlement, and 3 were left standing. At the Chandeliers, and in the center of the storm—where 200 fishermen dwelt—not a soul escaped. The dead were buried in trenches, where they were buried at all. In many instances, the young men who survived the shock of the storm were compelled to bury the rest of their families.

Reference http://www.victoriana.com/Hurricane/seaislandshurricane-2.html

Hurricane Katrina (August 29, 2005)

The most destructive hurricane ever to strike the United States, Hurricane Katrina was the 11th named storm in the busy 2005 hurricane season. The devastation in New Orleans and the surrounding Gulf Coast area cost over 1,800 lives, billions of dollars in damage, and catastrophic loss to the region's rich cultural heritage. The nation's most costly natural disaster, Katrina killed more than 1,600 people ... destroyed 200,000 Gulf Coast homes ... displaced about 1 million people. News reports place insured property damage at $25.3 billion in 1.7 million insurance claims—975,000 of them in Louisiana. According to 2000 U.S. Census data, over 450,000 people with disabilities reside along the section of the Gulf Coast that was affected by Hurricane Katrina. This website provides information for people with disabilities, their families and friends, and emergency responders who have to prepare and respond to emergencies and disasters.

http://uspolitics.about.com/od/katrina/i/katrina_first.htm

Great New England Hurricane (1938)

The hurricane dubbed by some as the "Long Island Express" made landfall over Long Island and Connecticut as a category 3 storm on September 21, 1938. The powerful hurricane decimated almost 9,000 buildings and homes, caused over 700 deaths, and reshaped the landscape of the south Long Island shore. The storm caused over $306 million in damage in 1938 dollars, which would equal about $3.5 billion in today's dollars. Over 690 people lost their lives during the Hurricane of 1938, due in part to the poor forecasts. The rapid forward motion of this storm, however, would make proper warning difficult even with today's technology. http://www.pbs.org/wgbh/amex/hurricane38/maps/index.html

San Francisco Earthquake (1906)

In the dark morning hours of April 18, 1906, the sleeping city of San Francisco was rocked by a massive earthquake. Walls caved in, streets buckled, and gas and water lines broke, allowing residents little time to take cover. The earthquake itself lasted less than a minute, but fires broke out across the city almost immediately, fueled by broken gas lines and a lack of water to put them out. Four days later, the earthquake and subsequent fire left more than half of San Francisco's population homeless, and had killed somewhere between 700 and 3000 people. At the time, 376 deaths were reported; the figure was fabricated by government officials who felt that reporting the true death toll would hurt real estate prices and efforts to rebuild the city; additionally, hundreds of casualties in Chinatown went ignored and unrecorded. Today, this figure has been revised to an estimate of at least 3,000.

http://history1900s.about.com/cs/sfearthquake/p/sfquake.htm

Georgia - South Carolina Hurricane (1881)

Hundreds of people were lost in this August 27th hurricane that struck the east U.S. coast at the juncture of Georgia and South Carolina, causing severe damage to Savannah and Charleston. The storm then moved inland, dissipating on the 29th over northwestern Mississippi, resulting in about 700 deaths. 1881 A deadly hurricane hit the coast of Georgia killing an estimate 700 people and leaving an unknown number homeless.

Tri-State Tornado in Missouri, Illinois and Indiana (1925)

Widely considered the most powerful and devastating tornado in American history, the Great Tri-State Tornado ripped through Missouri, Illinois and Indiana on March 18, 1925. It's 219-mile track killed 695 people, injured more than 2000, destroyed about 15,000 homes, and damaged more than 164 square miles. 243 people died in Murphysboro that day, 463 people required surgery, and many had limbs amputated even as the supply of anesthetics ran out. The tornado depressed the town's economy for 20 years. At the Longfellow Grade School, children were rushing out of the building as it collapsed, trapping roughly half of the 450 students. A block away, at the railroad repair yard, 35 men were killed .

In Murphysboro, the tornado claimed its greatest single disaster, where of the 127 people dead, most were women and children.

As the vortex crossed into Indiana at 4 pm, it hit its peak average speed of 73 mph and completely obliterated the town of Griffin—killing 25 and injuring 202. The tornado then veered off its straight-line course by 9 degrees, and at that point witnesses reported three separate funnels swirling within the larger maelstrom. The tornado was on a collision course with the town of Princeton, Ind., and when it hit 18 minutes later it had lost none of its power. It destroyed 25 percent of the town and killed 45 people. The tornado rolled on for another 12 minutes before disintegrating into the history books. By then, it had killed 695 people, injured thousands more, and demolished 15,000 homes.

http://www.weather.com/newscenter/specialreports/sotc/storm7/page1.html

PRIMARY SOURCE: Retrieved February 5, 2010 from the World Wide Web: http://genealogy.about.com/od/historic_disasters/tp/deadliest_us.htm

Group Therapy: An Approach to Disaster Intervention

Estelle L. Robinson, PhD

Case Manager, Crisis Detection Program
Director and Youth Build Counselor at International Relief and Development
U.S. Crisis Counselor for the Mississippi Department of Mental Health
Project Recovery Biloxi - Hurricane Katrina

The primary objective of disaster intervention is to help survivors realize that their feelings, thoughts, and behaviors are normal reactions to an abnormal event. Psychological impact is intensified and long lasting when at least two of the following factors are present (Picou, 2008)

- Extreme and widespread damage to property
- Perceived degree of ambiguous loss
- Extensive damage to community infrastructure and social fabric
- High prevalence of injury, loss of life, and/or threat to life
- Human negligence or pre-meditated intent

By listening to a survivor's story, a disaster counselor assesses where a survivor is on the Pessimism/Optimism Continuum (Table I) and then encourages the survivor to employ more optimistic coping strategies in order to take control of her/his recovery. The greater the perceived impact, the more pessimistic will be a survivor (Smallwood, 2007).

Table I. Pessimism/Optimism Continuum

Pessimism	**Optimism**
Denial	Reality
Victimhood	Responsibility
Powerlessness	Empowerment
Why?	How?
Doubt	Faith
Bitterness or Anger	Deliverance
Guilt	Self-forgiveness
Isolation	Connection
Avoidance	Courage
Depression	Grief

The prevailing mental health interventions have focused on individualized crisis counseling or Critical Incident Stress Management (Doherty, 2007 & Mitchell & Everly, 1995). as the interventions of choice. The terrorists attacks on the World Trade Center in New York City on September 11, 2001 (9/11), Hurricane Katrina's devastating destruction of the Mississippi Gulf Coast on August 29, 2005, and the breaching of the New Orleans, Louisiana levies on August 30, 2005 are community disasters, which suggest that some disaster survivors may need continued intervention and support.

Piper and Ogrodniczuk (2004) suggest that group therapy is the treatment of choice for bereavement, trauma reactions, and adjustment problems and is as efficacious as individual therapy. Literature reviews of group therapy have found evidence to suggest that group therapy is a beneficial and cost-effective approach for numerous intrapersonal and interpersonal issues (Burlingame, Fuhriman, & Johnson, 2004a, 2004b, Burlingame, MacKenzie, Strauss, 2004, Fuhriman & Burlingame, 1999, Markus & King, 2003, Piper and Ogrodniczuk, 2004).

All survivors benefit from sharing "Their Story" with fellow survivors, which provides an opportunity to "normalize" experiences and emotions, learn how others are coping and recovering as well as begin establishing a new equilibrium. Survivors may feel overwhelmed because pre-disaster coping strategies are ineffective, may have difficulty rationalizing the overwhelming physical destruction and ambiguous loss, expressing intense negative feelings, feel isolated, and have a tendency to avoid places, people, or activities that remind them of the distressing experience. Survivors may physically and/or emotional withdraw or experience emotional numbness. For these individuals the counseling group process will facilitate recovery.

Government funding for disaster mental health intervention is short lived. Duration of mental health intervention is contingent upon a survivor's perceived impact from the disaster. Ambiguous loss, the loss of intangible value—the emotional value a person has transferred onto physical objects, affects a survivor's resilience to recover. For some survivors awareness of ambiguous loss may be delayed for months or years after a disaster (Boss, 2006). A community network would facilitate acknowledgement and resolution of ambiguous loss.

Survivors need a community network to support each other throughout the long-term recovery process after disaster counselors have felt. Through group counseling a community support network could be developed that assures survivors that they are not alone and that they have a ready support system to help each other establish a new equilibrium.

When emotional reactions are intense survivors may be tempted to slide back into procrastination, isolation, and avoidance. To diminish such thoughts counselors need to help survivors interact with others in order to normalize their reactions, reframe self-talk, and facilitate resiliency to regain control of their lives. Social interaction offers a break from haunting memories, anxieties, and depressing thoughts, which plague survivors.

A group counseling intervention program should integrate psychoeducational and counseling group approaches. The objectives would be to first help survivors normalize their thoughts and feelings concerning how a disaster has affected their lives. Secondly, facilitate the recovery process by helping survivors identify their psychological strengths, and finally to encourage survivors to use their psychological strengths to adopt a more optimistic perspective toward recovery.

Psychoeducation will correct cognitive, emotional, and behavioral information deficits, thereby facilitating normalization of survivors' thoughts and feelings concerning the disaster. Additionally, effective coping skills will be acquired through experiential exercises, as well as homework assignments.

Focusing on resolving specific short-term issues, a counseling perspective will promote interactive feedback between co-leaders and survivors to provide support for self-exploration. The counseling group process will provide a supportive environment which will help survivors recognize their psychological strengths, provide interactive feedback to instigate behavioral change, develop more positive attitudes, and strengthen interpersonal skills. The dynamics of the counseling group process will facilitate the healing forces by providing an opportunity for survivors to discuss how the disaster has affected them. Experiential exercises will help survivors identify and express the full range of their feelings. The cohesion and trust generated amongst survivors will re-establish a sense of community. The resistance and conflict, which emerges in the group process will offer insight and discussion into the obstacles that are hindering recovery.

Applying newly acquired skills learned in the group process will expedite recovery.

About the Author

Estelle L. Robinson earned a doctoral degree in Experimental Psychology from the University of Southern Mississippi. Robinson's research was in developmental disabilities. From 1998 to 2005 Robinson was the President and Educational Director of Healthcare Administrative Services, a medical coding and billing school, located in Biloxi, Mississippi.

After losing the school in Hurricane Katrina, Robinson worked as a Crisis Counselor for the Mississippi Department of Mental Health's Project Recovery. As a crisis counselor of Project Recovery, Robinson managed a 17 member outreach team, provided crisis counseling to citizens of Harrison, Hancock, and Pearl River Counties, Mississippi, developed and implemented strategy plans to help alleviate Post Traumatic Stress Disorder (PTSD) and Adjustment Disorder, substance abuse, depression and anxiety, and assisted Hurricane Katrina survivors in resolving any and all issues directly and remotely associated with personal, community, and cultural destruction from a natural disaster.

Since the conclusion of Project Recovery in April of 2007 Robinson has served as a Case Manager, Crisis Detection Program Director, and Youth Build Counselor at International Relief and Development – U.S. As a Case Manager Robinson was responsible for obtaining financial assistance, procuring materials, as well as volunteer labor to rebuild homes in Hancock, Harrison, and Jackson Counties, Mississippi. In the capacity of Crisis Detection Program Director Robinson built and maintained relationships with local community and faith-based organizations with interests in advocating to reduce the suffering of vulnerable groups and provided resources needed for self-sufficiency and community sustainability, compiled a Disaster Psychological First-Aid Manual, coordinated, trained and managed a Disaster Psychological First-Aid team, orchestrated and managed a telephone disaster "Hot Line," and collected, analyzed, and disseminated relevant program data. As a Youth Build Counselor Robinson provided individual and group counseling to at-risk adolescents, and conducted life and career skills classes.

References

Boss, Pauline. (2006). *Loss, trauma, and resilience therapeutic work with ambiguous loss.* New York, NY. W.W. Norton & Company, Inc.

Burlingame, G.M., Fuhriman, A.J., & Johnson, J. (2004a). Current status and future directions of group therapy research. In J.L. DeLucia-Waack, D. Gerrity, C.R. Kalodner, & M.T. Riva (Eds.) *Handbook of group counseling and psychotherapy* (pp. 651-660). Thousand Oaks, CA: Sage.

Burlingame, G.M., G.M., Fuhriman, A.J., & Johnson, J. (2004b). Process and outcome in group counseling and psychotherapy: A perspective. In J.L. DeLucia-Waack, D. Gerrity, C.R. Kalodner, & M.T. Riva (Eds.) *Handbook of group counseling and psychotherapy* (pp. 49 - 61). Thousand Oaks, CA: Sage.

Burlingame, G.M., Mackenzie, K.R., & Strauss, B. (2004). Small group treatment: Evidence for Effectiveness and mechanisms of change. In M. Lambert (Ed.) Bergin & Garafield's *Handbook of psychotherapy and behavior change.* (5th ed., pp 647 – 696). New York: Wiley.

Doherty, G.W. (2007). *Crisis Intervention Training for Disaster Workers: An Introduction.* Laramie, WY: Rocky Mountain Disaster Mental Health Institute Press.

Fuhriman, A. & Burlingame, G.M. (1999). Does group psychotherapy work? In J.R. Price, D.R. Hescheles, & A.R. Price (Eds.) *A guide to starting psychotherapy groups.* (pp. 81 –98). San Diego, CA: Academic Press.

Markus, H.E., & King, D.A. (2003). A survey of group psychotherapy training during predoctoral psychology internship. Professional Psychology: Research and Practice, 34(2), 203 – 209.

Mitchell, J.T., Everly, G.S. (1995). *Critical incident stress debriefing: An operations manual for the prevention of trauma among emergency service and disaster workers* (2nd ed.). Baltimore, MD: Chevron.

Picou, Steven, J. (2008). *Preparing for chronic mental health impacts: Peer-listener training program.* 2008 Mental Health Summit. Mississippi Coast Interfaith Disaster Task Force. Biloxi, Mississippi.

Piper, W.E., & Ogrodniczuk, J.s. (2004). Brief group therapy. In J.L. DeLucia-Waack, D. Gerrity, C.r. Kalodner, & M.T. Riva (Eds.), *Handbook of group counseling and psychotherapy* (pp. 641-650). Thousand Oaks, CA: Sage.

Smallwood, Beverly. (2007). *This wasn't supposed to happen to me.* Nashville, TN Thomas Nelson.

Substance Abuse and Mental Health Services Administration (2005). *Adult assessment & referral tool.* (OMB NO. 0930-0270). Washington, D.C.: U.S. Government Printing Office.

Workshop: Healing the Wounds of Deployment: The 'Art' of Coming Home

Sandi J. Lloyd, Med, MA, LPC, ATR-BC

Manager for Banner Boswell and
Del E. Webb Medical Center's Outpatient Behavioral Health.

Abstract

The terror of the battlefield has always caused psychological, biological, and spiritual wounds. In today's military the wounds of being deployed not only affect the person being deployed but the family left behind. Four aspects of deployment will be addressed here: 1) leaving the family unit, 2) the new family dynamic developed by the family members left behind, 3) the return of the deployed person and 4) how the deployed person acclimates into the new family dynamic that developed while he/she was away. The case study will explore the use of Art as the modality for change and healing.

Background

Deployment does not affect just the person being deployed; deployment affects the entire family unit system. A myriad of issues may be experienced by the family such as grief, anger, fear, guilt, abandonment, and sadness that can lead to depression, anxiety, and stress. The purpose of this study was to examine some of the effects of deployment and how Art can be used as a healing modality within the family.

According to the Department of Defense (Shudro, 2005), since October 2001, more than 1.1 million men and women have served in Iraq and Afghanistan. A New England Journal of Medicine study (2004) reports that almost 2 out of every 10 US troops who have faced combat in Iraq may return with serious symptoms of depression, anxiety, or PTSD. Stress symptoms can include emotional numbness, sleep disturbances, depression, anxiety, irritability and outburst of anger. Feelings of intense guilt are also common according to a National Institute of Mental Health report (Hodge et al, 2004).

In a more recent study published in the *Archives of Internal Medicine* estimates that one-third of all returning veterans suffer from serious mental health and psychosocial disorders. Of those, 56% were diagnosed with more than one disorder including post traumatic stress disorder, depression, and substance abuse. The highest rate of mental health problems were among veterans in the 18-24 year old range and often those most exposed to front line combat (Reinberg, 2007).

Purpose

Deployment while it directly affects those individuals who are sent away, deployment also affects those who are left behind such as family, friends, and co-workers. For the family, the spouse or significant other that is left behind is now responsible for 100% of the family care (i.e., emotional, social, financial, etc.). Many of the same feelings that the deployed may experience are also felt by the family such as feelings of abandonment, anger, frustration, guilt, depression and anxiety.

These new feelings may in part be from the new family dynamic, as the members learn their new positions and responsibilities within the family unit. For some members it may be an opportunity to excel, to rise in the family unit and for others it may be seen as additional burdens to bear. In the extended family the members may feel a need to fill in for the missing family member emotionally financially or both. Friends and co-workers may miss the deployed person while they are absent. Other workers may have feelings of resentment as to having to pick up additional work that is being transferred to them in the person's absence.

The family unit goes through a minimum of two changes: the family member's deployment and the family members return. The saying "You can never go home" is true here. While yes, you can physically "go home", the person returning is different emotionally, spiritually, and often in the case of going to war, physically.

The deployed family member often expects to take up where he or she left off in the family causing the family member that has been in charge to relinquish certain duties. The family member left behind may or may not be ready to turn things back over to the returning member or may even resent the returning family member who is now disrupting the new family dynamic that was established in their absence. The returning family member may need to re-adjust not only to the new family dynamics but returning to civilian life and a job.

Interventions

To normalize the negative emotions expressed in the new family unit the following techniques may offer insight into the wounds of the returning veteran and those suffered by the family in his/her absence. The three types of therapy addressed here are Cognitive Behavioral Therapy (CBT), Role Playing and Art Therapy. Cognitive Behavioral Therapy allows the person to identify a situation, thoughts that the person is telling themselves and identification of feelings that are being experienced. In most cases the stressful situation cannot be changed as the situation has already taken place or is a projection into the future. In the case of deployment the stress may be thoughts associated with leaving the family, what was seen in battle or integrating into the new family unit. While none of these situations can be changed what the person is telling them self about these situations can. By disputing the thinking, new feelings can be experienced, giving to a new normal feeling within the family.

Role playing and Gestalt therapy can be helpful. Each of the spouses plays the role of the other. This allows each partner to have a better understanding of what it is to be in the other person's skin. In working with patients that are experiencing Post Traumatic Stress, the following interventions can be very beneficial in having the patient identify the stressor(s) of the situations.

1. Ask the client to identify their monsters and the monsters habitat. (This can be done with markers, paints, clay, and any medium that you have available

including magazines for collage work). Once the art work is done ask open ended questions to have the client share their thoughts and feelings regarding the images. The images may be realistic or abstract images. The art work becomes the center for discussion.

2. Another exercise is to have the client design a cape used to protect him/her from their monsters. Material for the cape can be a bed sheet that is cut up and markers can be used to decorate it. Once the cape is done the client would be asked to wear it, and to share how it feels. The images on the cape then become avenues for discussion. These images may then open doors that may never have been explored using other therapy modalities.
3. Collage work is often beneficial when working with PTSD clients. The client is asked to use pictures to represent sights, smells, and feelings that tend to bring on their PTSD. Once the client has completed the art work he or she is asked to create another piece of art that represents a distraction for when the PTSD thoughts come to mind. All the images would be explored.
4. PTSD often is coupled with stress in the client. To reduce stress, guided imagery is often helpful. Have the patient make a personal tape or have someone such as the therapist create one with soothing sounds and peaceful images. Learning to meditate, to be mindful of the quiet is also helpful. Deep breathing and pressure point techniques may also help reduce the stress in the PTSD client.

One intervention for re-establishing the family unit to a new workable norm is to ask each of the family members to journal the changes they have seen in the family unit. Creating a family crest can be done individually or as a family project. Another exercise is to have each of the family members draw a picture that represents the family before the family member was deployed and then what the family looks like now with the deployed person home. This exercise can provide a wealth of information as seen in this case study.

Grief which is about loss and not always about death is often experienced by those deployed and those left behind. Creating a Grief Journal is helpful with the client drawing or making comments on their feelings in the book. Topics that have been shown to be helpful is survivors guilt, the stages of grief, when, where, and why did this happen. Drawings' examining what their personal grief looks like and how it changes over time is also beneficial.

Anger is a stage of grief but is also displayed in clients with PTSD. Asking the client to express their anger artistically over a period of time is often helpful, whether the art is abstract or realistic. Once the image is created it becomes the focus of the discussion. The series of drawings or images is often a good way for the client to visually see how their anger images have changed over time and how their feelings have changed. Sometimes just pounding clay can be a good release or to make an image and then destroy it in a safe and appropriate way. Discussing how it feels to create something and then to destroy it often gives insight into additional feelings.

Art therapy is a modality that is used when words are not sufficient to express the emotions. It is not about being an artist or the actual piece of art that is created; it is about expressing emotions which then become the object for exploration. To give the reader an idea of how "Art" can heal the wounds of deployment the following Case Study is discussed.

Case Study

The following abbreviated notes involve a family in which the father is an Army Reservist who was deployed to Iraq for 13 months. The Army husband was a Sergeant, married with one daughter. His civilian job is working as a mortgage lender for a bank. The following depicts aspects of the therapy that took place over a three month period.

Meeting 1: Intake

After the husband and wife completed the intake process, they came together and discussed some of the family issues that were causing difficulties in their marriage. The couple decided that the wife would come first for a private session to be followed by the husband and then the child, a daughter, age 7.

Meeting 2: Individual art therapy

The wife discussed at this meeting how she felt while her husband was deployed and how upon his return his impressions of her had changed. Her drawing (Art #1) was created with markers.

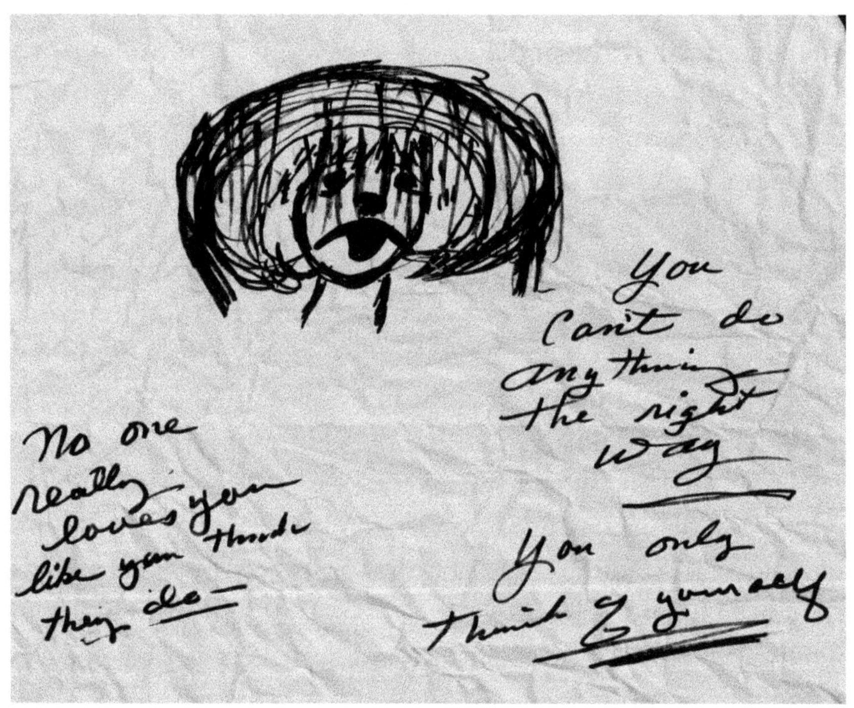

She noted that she felt in her husband's absence that "no one loved her", that everyone was just putting on a show for her. Upon her husband's return she felt that everything she had done in his absence was wrong, she could do nothing right, and that she was selfish, thinking only about herself. Using her art her negative self image and self talk was processed. Using CBT she was able to dispute these irrational beliefs allowing for new positive realistic thoughts and emotions to come into her life.

The husband, reluctant at first, to do a drawing but once assured it was not about his ability to draw the following image was created (Art #2, created using markers). His image displayed anger and had a monster appearance that he explained was how he felt when he was angry.

He was not so angry at what had happened at home during his absence, he was angry at all the coulda, woulda, shoulda's that he was feeling due to his deployment. Looking back on his 13 month tour he questioned everything he said, did, or didn't do. Using CBT to change some of his irrational thoughts and move into a place of acceptance the client was able to begin to look at his deployment differently, that he did the best he could with what he had at the time. His anger was addressed in almost every session to some extent over the case of therapy.

The daughter was asked upon her first visit to draw a picture of her family before her daddy went away. See Art #3.

Her picture shows her mom and dad holding hands, the sun is shining and their cat is next to her. The big tree is like the one in their yard. She used crayons to make her art. In asking her about her family the daughter said they use to be happy like her picture. She could not explain what was different now at home other than momma cries a lot and daddy is always mad and was scary.

Meeting 3:

Upon the third visit with the mother/wife, she was asked to draw a picture of what the family looked like before her husband was deployed, see Art #4 (crayons were used).

In the wife's/mother's drawing she put the family outside a home with a door and windows and flowers, grass and trees. She and her husband were drawn holding hands with the daughter a short distance from the mother. The wife reported that life seemed so less overwhelming before her husband deployed and that all was good. A short discussion on the family took place as to their interactions and what made their family life good.

The husband on his third visit, was asked to draw a picture of the family as he remembered them being before his deployment. See Art #5, he also used crayons.

He drew himself in his uniform with his wife next to him, holding hands and their daughter close to the mother. He was the only one of the family that drew himself with his uniform on. Discussion revolved around what they did as a family before he was deployed.

The daughter on her second visit was asked to draw a picture of her family now that her daddy was home. See Art #6, crayons were used.

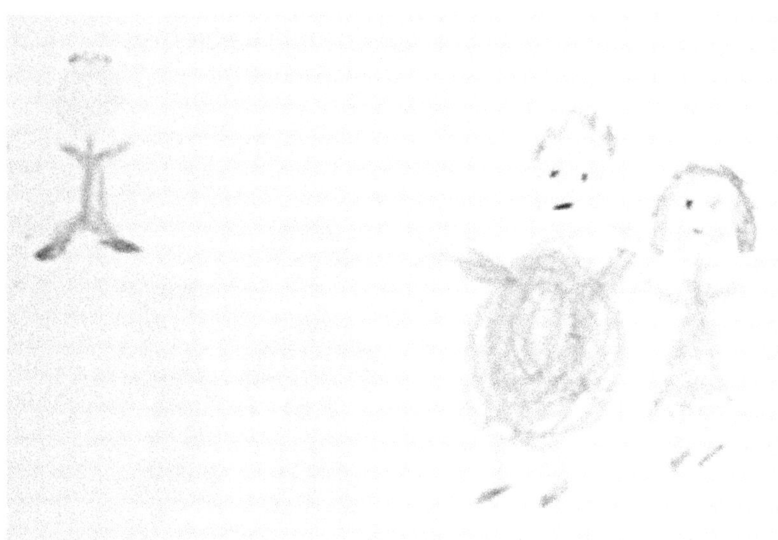

In this picture the child is standing next to her mother who now is round in appearance as the daughter reports her momma had gotten fat while her daddy was gone. Over to the left and smaller than the representation of the mother and daughter is the father. He has no features on his face. The daughter shared how she did not like being close to daddy because he was always mad and that she wished he would go away again.

Meeting 4

The mother, at this meeting was asked to draw the family as she saw it now, with her husband home. See Art #7, crayons were used.

She drew herself as larger in size and more rotund to show the weight she had gained. Her daughter was close to her and her husband was distant from her. The husband was as large as her but only have of him was drawn. In discussion of the images, the wife reported that she felt only half of her husband had returned, that the other half of him was still in Iraq. She did not like the half that had returned as he was so cross all the time and got angry about anything and everything as well as called her names at any given opportunity. The wife was given information about positive affirmations. She was able to create two and agreed to use them during the day when she felt she was not a good person.

The husband was asked to draw the family as he saw it now upon his return. See Art #8, crayons were used.

He drew himself again in his fatigues and larger than the rest of the family. He is separated from his wife who is holding hands with the daughter. He does not portray the wife as being overweight as it is difficult to tell from her clothes he has drawn. During the discussion the husband shares that because he does not sleep well that he has dark circles under his eyes and says he is haunted by what he as seen in Iraq. He shares it is hard to feel close to his family for many reasons, one being that he could not stand losing anyone else he cares for. He was asked if his behavior was not driving those he loved away. The client did not respond to this idea but this thought was addressed again in the therapy.

Meeting 5

The family was brought together and their family pictures shared. Each member was able to see the different perceptions of their family. Over the next several months, more and more issues were addressed between the family members and at last contact, while there were still some PTSD issues, the family once more saw themselves as a contented family unit.

Summary

Healing the wounds of deployment is often a long process for all involved. Using Art often allows for earlier breakthroughs tearing down resistance. A combination of meditation, CBT and art therapy proved to be a successful combination for the members of this family.

About the Author

Sandi Lloyd is the Manager for Banner Boswell and Del E. Webb Medical Center's Outpatient Behavioral Health programs in Sun City West, Arizona. She holds a Master's Degree from NAU in Educational Counseling, a Master's Degree in Professional Counseling from Ottawa University and a Certificate of Advance Graduate Studies in Art Therapy. She is currently writing her dissertation in Behavioral Medicine and will earn a Ph.D. in Psychology in 2010. She is an Arizona Licensed Professional Counselor and a Board Certified Art Therapist. Sandi has taught at several Phoenix area Colleges and Universities for the past 9 years. Sandi also owns a small publishing company and helps authors self-publish. She is married and has two grown sons. Sandi enjoys traveling with her husband, sailing, scuba diving, snow skiing, writing and painting.

References

Hodge, C. W., Castro, C. A., Messer, S. C., McGurk, D., Cotting, D. I., & Koffman, R. L. (2004). Combat duty in Iraq and Afghanistan, mental health problems, and barriers to care. The New England Journal of Medicine, 351, 13-22.

Reinberg, S. (2007). Mental health woes afflicts almost a third of Iraq, Afghan vets. Retrieved December 13, 2007, from http://www.healthfinder.gov/news/printnewstory.asp?docID=602675

Shudro, C. (2005). The unseen wounds of war. Retrieved December 10, 2007, from http://yalemedicine.yale.edu/ym_au05/war.html

Disasters: A Manifold Challenge for Social Science Practitioners and Researchers Alike

A.J.W. Taylor, PhD

Emeritus Professor of Psychology
Victoria University of Wellington, NZ

Abstract

Disasters of one kind or another have occurred since the dawn of history. In the early days, rulers sought explanations for their occurrence from prophets and seers. Since the days of enlightenment, and the emergence of scientific disciplines, governments have sought explanations other than the supernatural to account for them. This paper comments on the coverage and touches on some of the issues that have come the fore recently during the conduct of disaster research. In some ways, it might be 'a road less travelled.'

Introduction

Disasters are catastrophic events that seriously disrupt the everyday functioning of communities. In ancient times, they took the form of droughts, earthquakes, fires, floods, famines, hurricanes, plagues, storms, tsunamis, and volcanic eruptions, all of which brought massive loss of life, ruined seasonal crops, demolished habitats, threatened communities and cultural frameworks, and destroyed ancient civilizations.

The emergence of natural science in the 18th century as a rational pursuit in the acquisition of knowledge, brought the industrial revolution and accidents of major proportions to lengthen the catalogue of disasters. Early in the 20th century, with the further advance of science, technology and engineering, the list extended to include biological, chemical disasters in manufacturing plants and use of products, land/sea/air transportation accidents, and the use of gas and more sophisticated weaponry in warfare, including the atomic bomb.

In 1947, during the 'cold war' between former allies but ideologically different Western and Eastern political groups, the board of directors of the *Bulletin of the Atomic Scientists* at the University of Chicago dramatized the urgency of the day by invoking the notion of a doomsday clock. It warned that the closer the hands were to midnight, the closer was the proximity to a global disaster. With the specter of the atomic bomb devastation on Hiroshima and Nagasaki still in mind, it set the hands at seven minutes to midnight. Since then the board has moved the hands 19 times to reflect changes in the prevailing tension between nations and the wider acquisition of weapons of mass destruction. Currently, with the devastating effects of climate-change also coming into consideration, the hands stand at six minutes to midnight (cf. http://en/wikipedia. org/wiki/Doomsday_Clock - accessed 19 January 2010).[1]

Sometimes a sequence of disasters have been be discerned as links in a chain. In a challenging and detailed presentation, archaeological journalist David Keys (1988) argued that a catastrophe of mammoth proportions occurred in AD 535 that had world-wide consequences. Whether caused by an asteroid collision with the earth, a falling comet, or a tremendous volcanic eruption, it ejected millions of tons of debris into the atmosphere that enveloped both hemispheres in darkness for at least 18 months.[2] The loss of sunshine for so long a period destroyed all species of flora and fauna, some convincing evidence for which Keys was able to trace and present. Pulitzer Prize winning physiologist-cum-geographer Jared Diamond (1999; 2005) followed the same route, with two commendable tomes describing the linkage between a multitude of different kinds of disaster that affected the rise and fall of many civilizations.

Redoubtable sociologist Thomas E. Drabek (1986) was more concerned with the conceptual of disasters than the consequential interactions between them He synthesized nearly 1,000 reports of different disasters, and produced an integrated model showing four relatively distinct phases and six somewhat distinct system levels. The phases were of preparedness, response, recovery and mitigation, each of which had two subsidiaries. The system levels differed according to their focus on individuals, groups, emergency organizations, entire communities, society at large, or the wider international scene. The resulting 8 x 6 matrix provided a comprehensive overview of the field of disasters, with leads to different topics of concern.

Notable social scientist Kai Erikson (1994) was also conceptually interactive, but less expansive. Prompted to support community plaintiffs seeking compensation in four different types of disaster, he drew attention to three significant matters that researchers needed to address. The first was a theoretical model with which to understand the remarkable similarity in the adversity suffered by individuals. The second was the inclusion of community and cultural dimensions in the model. The third was an appeal for researchers to develop methods that would encourage victims to reveal the richness of their experience, instead of producing responses to predetermined questionnaires providing objectivity at the expense of validity. In doing so, he was unafraid of risking his reputation as a scientist by registering subjective factors, arguing that, in the disaster field at least, natural scientists and technologists had social responsibilities.

Failure to hearken to those key factors, for whatever reason, led many researchers to overlook the study of man-made disasters that brought severe and continuing disruption into the lives of countless thousands of people and produced bitter reactions on many fronts. Examples of such include white-collar criminality (cf. Sutherland 1949), devotion to free-

---

[1] To its credit, the editorial board of *Disaster: Journal of Disaster Studies, Policy & Management*, 2006, 30, devoted the entire volume to articles on climate change. The issue is very controversial, with stakes on both sides clouding the facts. As at 25 January 2010, the presentation of front-man Al Gore for one side could be seen at http://www.youtube.com/watch?v=Jxi-OlkmxZ4, and that of front-man John Coleman for the other at http://www.kusi.com/home/78477082.html?video=pop&t=a.

[2] In comparison with such work, and as an invited contributor to the chapter, without modesty I can say Harrison Taylor & Wichman's (2009) prognostication on the effect of an asteroid falling on the earth, is slight!

market economic policy (cf. Ian Taylor, 1990: Reich, 1991), and the resurgence of international terrorism (cf. Silke, 2003, pp. xv-xx1).

In the last two decades, the consequences have been astronomical. Firstly, the misery from fraudulent schemes perpetrated by the scions of commercial respectability still reverberates.[3] Secondly, the worship of 'free-market' economic theory allowed corporations to place monetary values far above the livelihood of individuals and the well-being of local communities (cf. Korten, 1996: Bakan, 2004).[4] In 1995 the International Federation of Red Crescent and Red Cross Societies (IFRC&RCS) expressed concern about the 'disaster inducement work of powerful self-promoting economic and political groups (IFRC&RCS, 1995, p.52), and three years later it included specific areas of socio-economic dislocation in its map of relief operations (IFRC&RCS, 1998, p. 188).[5] The global extension of the 'free market' led the World Commission on the Social Dimension of Globalization (2004, p. vii) to preface its report with a dire warning about the economic disparities that had worsened the lot of poorer nations, lest 'the world we all share slide into further spirals of political turbulence, conflicts, and wars.' It declared:

> 'The governance of globalization must be based on universally shared values and respect for human rights. Globalization has developed in an ethical vacuum, where market success and failure have tended to become the ultimate standard of behavior, and where the attitude of "the winner takes all" weakens the fabric of communities and societies.' (WCSDG, p.7).

Thirdly, terrorism, the strategy adopted by a militant minority to achieve political ends, became more complex. It focused on nodal points such as communication centers, food and water supplies, power grids, and transport networks, to maximize damage and disruption for the civilian population of a target country (cf. Lacquer, 1987; Silke, 2003). Soon after the terrorist attack of September 11, 2001 on the World Trade Center in New York (cf. *The 9/11 Commission Report*, n.d), president of the World Bank, James D Wolfenson, reiterated his concern that poverty and inequality were at the root of global ills that generate terrorism

---

[3] Consider the debacles of BCCI, Barings Bank, Andersons and Enron Energy, Xerox, Worldcom, Merril Lynch in the USA, insider trading at Lloyds of London, Elf Acquitane in France, LG Card in Korea, Akold in the Netherlands, Parmenter Corporation in Italy, Allied Irish Bank, Ariadne, Reid Murray and HIH Insurance in Australia and JBL, Equity Corporation and Ansett in New Zealand. The flush of deregulation had led many financial companies to abandon prudence in their dealings, and to become the respondents in civil action, if not the accused in criminal proceedings. Currently in New Zealand, five big companies in liquidation, and a few others, are in that position (cf. *Dominion Post*, 27 January 2010). They have caused untold damage to the security of thousands of employees and investors alike.

[4] Aid worker Giles Bolton (2007) provides a gritty first-hand account of the futile attempts by leading international agencies to improve the living standards of many African nations. He shows how the Western belief in the allocation of money to solve all basic problems, without first involving countries in assessing their basic needs and in developing administrative infrastructure and services to meet them, has been the constant recipe for disaster. He traces the interventions from imperialist days to the present, arguing that the disjunction between the assumptions and expectations of the donors and the recipients need substantially to be changed.

[5] The most recent report of Refugees International shows that in 2008 there were 15.2 million refugees in the world, 26 million people displaced within their own countries, 12 million with no legal bond of nationality within any state (http://www.refintl.org/get-involved/helpful-facts-25%2526-figures accessed 24 January 2010). Although it did not specify the economic status of refugees, it would be foolish to think that without work, property and possessions, their level of subsistence was other than precarious.

(Sullivan, 2002), and Secretary-General of the United Nations, Kofi Annan, appealed for member countries to adopt a common outlook of global citizenship with humanitarian as well as economic concerns.

Subsequently the United Nations General Assembly (2005) endorsed the WCSDG theme, and it urged member countries to redress their priorities to avoid further catastrophe. On the 10th August of the same year, Paul Hunt, a human rights legal advisor to the United Nations[6], addressed the School of Government at Victoria University on the abuse of economic, social and cultural rights, and he put it among the most important and challenging issues of the day. The very next week, at a National Counter Terrorism Capability Seminar in the same place, political analyst Kumar Ramakrishna (2005) of Nan Yang Technological University[7] described the interaction of three main roots of terrorism as being a striving for political ascendancy, the elaboration of an ideology, and a pervasive discontent with the status quo reflecting social injustice.

Warnings and appeals to governments to address the causes went unheeded. A monetary 'melt-down' ensued that has still to be rectified.[8] Under the guise of short-term expediency, and the fear of annihilation provoked to induce compliance, all three kinds of man-made disaster revived authoritarian and belligerent policies in countries that professed to be democratic. Currently, to paraphrase Marcellus' observation in *Hamlet*, all is not well in the state of Denmark.

The argument is not that disaster researchers should necessarily become involved actively in examining such macro-issues, but that they should support researchers in whose domain they lie, and take the matters into account as they pursue the micro-issues for which they have acquired expertise. More than that, they should be alert to long-standing issues in their own domain, and to fresh issues that come to their notice and have untold implications.

Micro-Issues In Disaster Research

Micro issues can be either standard or novel. Standard issues are those covered either during academic and professional training or in post-graduate updating. They involve epistemology, methodology, methods, the reliability and validity of scales for the target population and expected problems, the appropriateness of statistical procedures, appraisal of previous endeavors, logistical support, ethics, and security concerns during the promotion of the research. Novel issues are those that come to attention serendipitously during the conduct of research and require detailed consideration later.

With regard to the standard issues, in disaster research social scientists would do well to avoid Scylla and Charybdis in their devotion either to objectivity or to subjectivity in their methodology and methods. The one leads to rigor mortis rather than rigor, and the other to sloppy conclusions. They have to make sure that their strategies, methods, techniques, and data manipulation are appropriate for the topic in question, rather than representing either a slavish devotion to the gold standard of experimental method learned in a sterile laboratory,

---

[6] (cf. http://www.essex.ac.uk/human_rights_centre/research/rth/docs/Paul_Hunt_profile.pdf).

[7] (cf. http://www.rsis.edu.sg/about_rsis/staff_profiles/Kumar.html).

[8] Having said that, I should point out that on the investment front, Harry S. Dent (2009) is supremely confident that the careful observance of the long-term cyclical fluctuations in stocks, real estate and commodities, will alone indicate the route for recovery.

or the arrogant abuse of freedom to design research according to the project on hand. Lessons are to be learned from medical 'experiments' in Auschwitz concentration camps (Russell, 1955), the CIA sponsored sensory deprivation studies at McGill University and elsewhere in the 1960s (Victorian, 1996), and from professional codes of ethics that give priority to the welfare of research participants over the concerns of narrowly-focused experimenters (Pappworth, 1967). Lessons are also to be gained from the intellectual nonsense that physicist Alan Sokal fabricated in 1996 and the well-meaning post-modernist journal of social science, Social Text, took on trust and published.[9]

The epistemological issue is not confined to conflict between academic disciplines. In social science: there is constant and long-standing tension between those who aspire for recognition as pure scientists and others content to apply their skills in the service of mankind. In psychology, for example, in 1968 US Navy Commander Newell H Berry presented a forthright paper on the issue to the London Conference of the British Psychological Society. He was circumspect about the relevance, methodology and outcome of a sample of some 4,000 research reports that his government had sponsored from psychologists.[10] Kerry Chamberlain (2009) addressed similar gatherings of the British and the New Zealand Psychological Societies on the same topic to the same effect recently. The only difference was that modern researchers had a compendium of more sophisticated questionnaires and statistical procedures at their disposal that does not allow them to cover their inadequacies with the lame excuse that 'more research is required'.[11]

The catalog of novel micro-issues emerging from disaster research to require attention includes:

- the adequacy of mortuary facilities and services
- the perceptual defense spontaneously adopted by body recovery workers
- the provision of psychological first-aid for casualties rather than victims
- the timing and efficacy of subsequent interventions
- recognizing the philosophical component of personality and group membership
- enhancing the placebo effect and fostering self-help, and
- encouraging the media to adopt a responsible role in post-disaster management.

To some extent, the World Health Organization (2004) met the first of those issues by setting out the requirements of temporary field-cam mortuaries and emphasizing the socio-cultural obligations of handling of human remains. But it left aside the perceptual defense that emergency personnel adopted when handling carnage, and the inadequacy of existing

---

[9] The editors of the Journal, sociologists David Bloor, Barry Barnes and Bruno Latour, had advocated the use of novelty to break the fetters of experimental method that were inappropriate for their discipline. The physicist Alan Sokal took them at their word and presented a paper that parodied their intentions, to the embarrassment of many scholars.

[10] I heard the presentation, and I have a copy of the unpublished paper.

[11] As an occasional reviewer for international journals, I have been saddened by the disparity between the inability of some researchers to gather useful data and their outstanding ability to process it. More than that, a free for all seems to occur after major widespread disasters such as earthquakes and tsunamis: everyman and his dog get loose as expert disaster researchers. It was much the same after the 9/11, 2001 terrorist attack on the World Trade Centre in New York.

mortuary facilities in metropolitan areas that originally aroused my interest (cf. Taylor, 1984). Doherty (2007; 2010) and the joint National Child Traumatic Stress Network and National Center for PTSD (2008) met the second with helpful guidelines on the provision of psychological first aid for disaster victims, without addressing the need to collect data for research purposes.[12] The latter is important, because in the case of emergency personnel, if not primary casualties, data showed that 'one-shot' debriefing did not prevent the emergence of PTSD symptoms, as its exponents had claimed (cf. Rose Bisson Churchill & Wesseley, 2010).

The third should come into play once any threats to life and limb are reduced. It requires health professionals not to give undue attention immediately either to any particular psychological symptoms that casualties might report, or to signs they might themselves observe, but to allow casualties a few days grace in which they might begin to use their inner strength and regain composure. Within the limits of common sense, the time for them to register features of psychopathology comes later, should casualties find intrusive thoughts, avoidance behavior, and state of high arousal beginning seriously to interfere with their everyday lives (cf. Young, Ford, Ruzek, Friedman, & Gusman, 1998; Raphael, 2000).

Delay should not put the casualties unduly at risk because, as the World Health Organization (WHO) (2003, p. 4) stated:

> 'Most acute mental health problems during the acute emergency phase are best managed without medication following the principles of 'psychological first-aid' (i.e. listen, convey compassion, assess needs, ensure basic physical needs are met, not force talking, ...mobilise company from preferably family or significant others, encourage but do not force social support, protect from further harm.'

However, no matter how prestigious the authority recommending treatments, health professionals themselves remain accountable for the potency and impotency of their interventions, and for that reason they and their organizations will have to address the difficult question of designing appropriate procedures for evaluating the quality of their work

The resolution, rather than a rational appraisal of the clinical evidence, might depend more on irregular and extraneous factors. Journalist Tara McKelvey (2009) has just drawn attention to the most appropriate treatment for US soldiers suffering psychiatric disorder from their service in Afghanistan and Iraq (cf. Hoge Castro Messer McGurk Cotting & Koffman, 2004). She cited the severe existential dilemma of an Army Chaplain from fighting a war for which the moral justification (i.e. weapons of mass destruction at the ready) was baseless, and his reactions to the growing reliance of the army to use religion to fill the 'spiritual abyss' of those whose faith in a benevolent God was challenged by the carnage they had either witnessed or in which they had participated. She argued, quite rightly in my view, that such use of religion was questionable. The matter has yet to become a live issue among health practitioners, let alone disaster researchers.

Personally, as a Quaker and a clinical psychologist I am not averse to the interplay of religion and therapy. It reflects a belief that there is inner strength, that of God, in everyone, and a commitment to O'Donohue's (1989) metaphysician/scientist/practitioner model for appraising

---

[12] Although Leigh Smith's chapter in Paton Violanti Dunning and Smith's (2004) comprehensive handbook on the management of traumatic stress deals with the assessment of risk, rather than the outcome of interventions per se, it introduces some of the issues common to both domains.

human behavior. The need for such a combination came clear to me early in my career when I ran therapy groups for prisoners (Taylor, 1964). In that setting, behavior change depended on offenders discerning the unique combination of emotional, legal, moral, religious, and social factors behind their crimes, and their developing a higher purpose in life and attachments with which to pursue it.

The importance of value systems also became clear to me when I encountered a few emergency workers after an air crash in the Antarctic and survivors of a cyclone in the South Pacific, who attributed the disasters to fundamentalist Christian beliefs in Divine punishment for the unspecified moral transgression of the whole of their communities (Taylor & Frazer, 1981; Taylor, 1991). In both instances they were searching for explanations to account for the tragic loss of life. Their search stopped short of reflecting on either anxiety over the denial of death (Becker, 1973) or its antithesis, the desire to hasten death as suicide bombers on a Jihad (http://www. religioustolerance.org/isl_jihad.htm - accessed 29 January 2009: Ali, 2003). But it had confirmed their operating belief system—in one case for the few individuals holding the beliefs, and in the other for the cohesion of the community in an isolated part of the world.

In neither case did I think it appropriate to question the beliefs that were expressed, although on the different occasions I did just suggest that the victims of the air crash might have belonged to other faiths, and that more appropriate explanations for the recurrent cyclones might be found in climatology and oceanography rather than theology. I left aside for later consideration, the points that the God of the *New Testament* would have offered acceptance and forgiveness rather than extermination, the same God would not have punished the many for the behavior of a few, and the acceptance of scientific explanations would not diminish the spiritual core of religious belief (Taylor, 1999).

Fostering the placebo effect deserves a mention, except for those that have either died from the calamity or suffered irrevocably in some other equally significant way. It fosters hope for recovery through the positive power of the placebo effect and simultaneously negates the stultifying power of its counterpart, the *nocebo* effect. It is consistent with the adaptation of Nietzsche's saying—'that which does not kill me [might make] me strong'. The same holds true for preferring the term 'casualty' rather than 'victim' for those whose lives have been affected adversely by exposure to catastrophe. It implies the membership of a provisional rather than a permanent category. It applies to people that have survived the initial impact of a life-threatening event of some magnitude, and who might even find benefit psychologically from having survived catastrophic experience (cf. Tedeschi, Park, and Calhoun, 1998). In fact, and without going quite so far as to say with Samuel Johnson that 'when a man knows he is to be hanged in a fortnight, it concentrates his mind wonderfully', there is truth in the saying that the awareness of death causes a re-examination of value systems (Ursano, Tzu-Cheg, & Fullerton, 1992).

Finally, a responsible role for the media came into consideration because of the heightened impact those organizations have on the well-being and responsiveness of their audiences. Journalist Langewiesche's (2003) fulfilled his commission in book form admirably. Too often, his colleagues harass casualties to bleed their emotions, either to provoke extremes of either compassion or anxiety in their audiences, or worse, to satisfy the prurient. Invariably their programmes raise critical audience ratings that advertisers keenly seek. One study showed that New Yorkers directly exposed to the 9/11 attacks on the World Trade Center who viewed the televised images of that event more than seven times, were more likely to suffer posttraumatic stress disorders and or depression than a control group (Ahern Galea Resnick Kilpatrick Bucuvalas Gold & Vlahov, 2002). (It would also be interesting to know the effect on viewers whose only exposure to the calamity was indirect.)

Down here in New Zealand the crucial 15 minute tape of the planes colliding into the twin towers and the immediate aftermath was played almost hourly for two-days. In the words of a television announcer, quite irresponsibly to my mind, it was designed to create 'an indelible impression' on viewers. Also, days after an earthquake, an irresponsible radio announcer said that the emergency responders had not begun to count the bodies in a city some 150 kms from epicenter. It led agitated relatives in both hemispheres to seek confirmation that their loved ones were safe. In fact today, years after the event, the bodies have *still* not been counted, because there were none to be counted! Most recently after reports of a tsunami in nearby Samoa, a TV presenter persistently inquired whether the local populace had begun to panic—as if they were expected to panic at some final stage.

My response was to challenge the arms of the news media to fulfill the once responsible and respectable function of the 'fourth estate', at least in reporting disasters (Taylor, 2006). Suffice to say, the Ministry of Civil Defence and Emergency Management let contracts with the news media, but it seems to have left the organizations to train their own announcers to implement them.

Conclusion

Others will have their own catalogs of dissonance between the ideal and the actual in the conduct of disaster research. If the volley presented here gives them encouragement to share their thoughts and work on remedies, it will have more than served its purpose.

References

Ahern, J., Galea, S., Resnick, H., Kilpatrick, D., Bucuvalas, M., Gold, J., & Vlahov, D. (2002). Television images and psychological symptoms after the September 11 terrorist attack. *Psychiatry*, 65, 4, 289-300.

Ali, T. (2003). *The clash of fundamentalisms: Crusades, Jihads and modernity.* London: Verso.

Bakan, J. (2005). *The corporation: The pathological pursuit of profit and power.* London: Constable.

Baker, G.W. & Chapman, D.W. (Eds). (1962). *Man and society in disaster.* New York: Basic Books.

Becker, E. (1973). *The denial of death.* New York: The Free Press.

Berry. N.H. (1968) 1879 and all that. Invited paper for the London Conference of the British psychological Society. 18 December. private circulation. pp. 20.

Bolton, G.B. (2008). *Aid and other dirty business: An insider reveals how good intentions have failed the world's poor.* London: Ebury Press.

Cantril, H. (1947). The invasion from Mars. In T.M. Newcomb & E.L. Hartley. (Eds). *Readings in social psychology.* (ch.15). New York: Henry Holt.

Chamberlain, K. (2009). Constructing knowledge in contemporary psychology: Some critical comments. *Psychology Aotearoa*, 1, 1, 47-52.

Dent, H.S. (2009). *The great depression ahead: How to prosper in the crash that follows the greatest boom in history.* Melbourne: Schwartz.

Diamond, J. (1999). *Guns, germs, and steel: The fates of human societies.* New York: Norton.

Diamond, J. (2005). *Collapse: How societies choose to fail or survive.* London: Penguin.

Doherty, G.W. (2007). *Crisis intervention training for disaster workers: An introduction.* Laramie WY: Rocky Mountain Disaster Mental Health Institute Press.

Doherty, G.W. (2010)/*From crisis to recovery: Strategic planning for response, resilience, and recovery.* Laramie WY: Rocky Mountain Disaster Mental Health Institute Press.

Drabek, T.E. (1986). *Human system responses to disaster: An inventory of sociological findings.* New York: Springer-Verlag.

Drabek, T.E. (2010). *The human side of disaster.* London: CRC/Taylor & Francis.

Erikson, K. (1994). *A new species of trouble: Explorations in disaster, trauma, and community.* New York: Norton.

Harrison, A. A., Taylor A. J. W. & Wichman, H. (2009). Behavioural factors and planetary defense. In I. Bekey. (Ed.). *Dealing with the Threat to Earth from Impact by Asteroids and Comets.* (ch.6). International Academy of Astronautics.

Hoge, C.W., Castro, C.A., Messer, S.C., McGurk, D., & Cotting, D.I., & Koffman, R.L. (2004). Combat Duty in Iraq and Afghanistan, Mental Health Problems, and Barriers to Care. *New England Journal of Medicine*, 351, 13-22 - accessed 28 January 2010 from http://content.nejm.org/cgi/content/full/351/1/13.

Keys, D. (1999). *Catastrophe: An investigation into the origins of the modern world.* London: Century.

Korten, D.C. (1996). *When corporations rule the world.* West Hartford CT: Kumarian Press & Berret-Koehler.

Langewiesche, W. (2003). *American ground: Unbuilding the World Trade Center.* New York: North Point.

Laquer, W. (1987). *The age of terrorism.* Boston: Little Brown & Co.

McKelvey, T. (2009). God, the Army, and PTSD. *New York Times,* 17 December.

Prince, S.H. (1920). *Catastrophe and social change, based upon a sociological study of the Halifax disaster. New York:* Columbia University. Doctoral dissertation.

National Child Traumatic Stress Network and National Center for PTSD (2008). *Psychological First Aid: Field Operations Guide.* (2nd edn.). Washington DC: Authors.

O'Donohue, W. (1989). The (even) bolder model: The clinical psychologist as a metaphysician-scientist-practitioner. *American Psychologist,* 44, 12, 1460-1468.

Pappworth, M.H. (1967). *Human guinea pigs: Experiments on man.* Harmondsworth: Pelican Books.

Ramakrishna, K. (2005). The 'root causes' of terrorism: A new approach to an old problem. Paper delivered to the August National Counter Terrorism Capability Seminar, Victoria University of Wellington, N Z.

Raphael, B. (2000). *Disaster mental health handbook: An educational resource for health professionals involved in disaster management.* North Sydney: New South Wales Centre for Mental Health.

Reich, R.B. (1991). *The work of nations: A blueprint for the future.* London: Simon & Shuster.

Rose, S.C., Bisson, J., Churchill, R., & Wesseley, S. (2010). Psychological debriefing for preventing post-traumatic stress disorder (PTSD). *Cochrane Database of Systematic Reviews 2002, 2, Art. No.: CD000560. DOI 10.1002/14651858. CD000560* - accessed 29 January 2010.

Russell, Lord E.F.L. (1955). *The scourge of the swastika: A short history of Nazi war crimes.* (7th edn). London: Cassell.

Silke, A. (Ed.). (2003). *Terrorists, victims and society.* New York: Wiley.

Smith, L.M. (2004). Measuring protective behaviours for perceived risks of hazards. In D. Paton, J.M. Violanti, C. Dunning, L. & Smith. (Eds). (2004). *Managing traumatic stress risk: A proactive approach.* (ch.4). Springfield ILL: Thomas.

Sokal, A. (1996). Transgressing the boundaries: Towards a transformative hermeneutics of quantum gravity. *Social Text,* 46/47, 217-252 - retrieved1 November 2004 from http://www.physics.nyu.edu/faculty/sokal/index.html.

Sutherland, E.H. (1949). *White collar crime.* New York: Holt Reinhart & Winston.

Taylor, A.J.W. (1984). Architecture and society: Disaster studies and human stress. *Ekistics: The Problems & Science of Human Settlements,* 308, 446-451.

Taylor, A.J.W. (1990). A pattern of disasters and victims. *Disasters: The Journal of Disaster Studies & Management,* 14:4, 291-300.

Taylor, A.J.W. (1999). Value-conflict arising from a disaster. *Australasian Journal of Disaster & Trauma Studies.* http://www.massey.ac.nz/~trauma/issues/1999-2/taylor.htm.

Taylor, A.J.W. (2000). Tragedy and trauma in Tuvalu. *Australasian Journal of Disaster & Trauma Studies.* http://www.massey.ac.nz/~trauma/issues/2000-2/taylor.htm.

Taylor, A.J.W. (2003). Bringing 'complex terrorism' and 'corporate malfeasance' into a classification schema for disasters. *Australian Journal of Emergency Management*, 18, 1, 27-34.

Taylor, A.J.W. (2006). Consolidating the role of the fourth estate in disaster work. *International Journal of Mass Emergencies & Disasters*, 14, 1, 145-167.

Taylor, A.J.W. (2007). Defusing terrorism of terror. In B. Bongar, L. Beutler, P. Zimbardo, L.M. Brown, & J.N. Breckenridge. (Eds). *The psychology of terrorism.* (ch. 24). Oxford University Press.

Taylor, A.J.W., & Frazer, A.G. (1981). *Psychological sequelae of Operation Overdue following the DC10 air crash in Antarctica.* Wellington: Victoria University, pp. 72.

Taylor, A.J.W. Nailatikau, S., & Walkey, F.H. (2002). A hostage trauma assignment in Fiji. *Australasian Journal of Disaster & Trauma Studies,* http://www.massey.ac.nz/~trauma/issues/2002-2/taylor.htm.

Taylor, I. (Ed.). (1990). *The social effects of Free Market policies: An international text.* New York: Harvester Wheatsheaf.

Tedeschi, R.D., Park, C.L., & Calhoun, L.G. (Eds). (1998). *Posttraumatic growth: Positive changes in the aftermath of crisis.* Mahwah NJ: Erlbaum.

The 9/11 Commission Report: Final report of the National Commission on Terrorist attacks upon the United States. (n.d). New York Norton.

United Nations. (2005). In larger freedom: Towards development, security, and human rights for all. Report of the Secretary-General. A/59/2005. New York. pp. 62.

Ursano, R.J., Tzu-Cheg, K., & Fullerton, C.S. (1992). Post traumatic disorder and meaning: Structuring human chaos. *Journal of Nervous and Mental Disease*, 180, 12, 756-759.

Victorian, A. (1996). United States, Canada, and Britain: Partners in mind control - accessed 11 April 2005 from http://www.peace.ca/mindcontroloperations.htm.

World Health Organisation. (2004). *Management of dead bodies in disaster situations.* Disaster Manuals and guidelines Series # 5. Washington DC.

Young, B.H. Ford, J.D. Ruzek, Friedman M.J., & Gusman, F.D. (1998). Disaster mental health service: A guidebook for clinicians and administrators. White River Junction VT: Department of Veterans Affairs.

Psychological Growth and The Value of the Phenomenological Narrative for Healthy Reintegration of Returnees and Their Families

Lynne McCormack, Trauma Psychologist

Centre for Trauma, Resilience and Growth (CTRG),
School of Sociology and Social Policy,
University of Nottingham, Nottingham NG7 2RD UK

Abstract

For the many individuals involved in modern international conflicts and disasters, similarities exist in how individuals make meaning of complex international events and homecoming. Many are plagued by personal moral doubt and self blame that result in isolation from intimate others, feelings of rejection and difficulties in social reintegration. Post mission reintegration processes are important determinants of psychological wellbeing and can facilitate honest self evaluation for redefining renewed altruistic identities. As such, this article highlights: 1. the importance of organizational role in psychosocial care of their staff on return from mission to reduce long-term social disruption and psychological distress; 2. the value of subjective, phenomenological interpretation in contrast to a medical model interpretation of psychopathology in working with returnees. Early research is discussed that supports the opportunity for vicarious growth in carers and therapists. Similarly, it explores the opportunity for psychological growth through honest self evaluation and self reparation in those exposed to complex and threatening international events.

Key words: Phenomenological interpretation, psychological growth following complex trauma, modern international conflicts, vicarious growth

Introduction

Modern struggles are fundamentally global social movements rather than political struggles. As such they will resist the individualistic thought of democratic logic and the force of foreign armies. Similarly, the increasing de-territorialized nature of ethical rather than political conflicts means that combatant war is more likely to be indiscriminate and without real and visible enemies (Chandler, 2009) offering no immunity for civilian nationals, international support groups or humanitarian personnel from warring parties and armies. Similarly, such conflicts invariably create moral confusion for many of the young soldiers involved. As a consequence individuals involved in these conflicts can be left unable to intimately reconnect with loved ones (McCormack, 2009; McCormack, Hagger & Joseph, 2009) and be plague with complex traumatic memories that can unexpectedly trigger involuntary arousal and fragmented flashbacks throughout a lifetime (Brewin, Dalgleish & Joseph, 1996).

However, until a social formula for co-existence redefines our communication across cultures and nations many will experience both the positive and negative consequences of international conflict. Fortunately, the potential for posttraumatic growth (Tedeschi and Calhoun, 1995; 1996) following extreme adversity is now recognised following a wide range of traumatic life events (for reviews see Helgeson, Reynolds & Tomich, 2006; Joseph & Linley, 2008; Prati & Pietrantoni, 2009). Similarly there are a few studies that suggests personal benefits and positive changes can also arise through vicarious exposure to trauma both as the partner of a veteran or as a trauma therapist (Arnold, Calhoun, Tedeschi & Cann, 2005; Brady et al., 1999; Dekel, 2007; Linley, Joseph & Loumidis, 2005; Pearlman & Saakvatne, 1995; Schauben & Frazier, 1995; Shiri, Wexler, Alkalay et al, 2008).

Although nationals of countries afflicted by global conflicts often work closely alongside non-national support, this article is concerned mainly with the experiences of non-nationals and their reintegration to their own societies on homecoming. It reflects on the complex interplay between psychological, social and cultural factors that challenge psychological wellbeing of such groups caught in the turmoil of war and disaster. I comment on organizational responsibility to the individual returnee, their families and society and the opportunity for positive change and psychological growth in the returnee, and vicarious growth for partners and trauma therapists.

From my own work as a trauma therapist and researcher of varying groups exposed to war, genocide and natural disasters, and my personal experience working in locations of war and complex emergencies, I have come to recognize that although organizational and mission statements differ substantially between groups, the individual experience can be one of threat to personal moral integrity and sense of self when confronted with catastrophic human suffering. Individual resources for growth out of extreme adversity however can be metamorphic. This does not appear to be limited to western cultures and comment is made on the use of psychosocial programs cross-culturally.

The Burden of Modern Global Crises on The Individual

There are many groups that currently participate in modern international conflicts: young soldiers, peacekeepers, humanitarian aid workers, civilian medical staff, entertainers, journalists or logistic support personnel. For each, integration of their experiences on mission and on return home is often distinctly different yet there are many similarities in the individual moral and personal experience. Similarly, supporting their reintegration into society may hold common threads for the therapist and intimate partners.

Understanding the impact of modern global crises on those who contribute when needed to the distress of others is crucial to our survival as civilized societies. When individuals risk their lives in the care of others, they should expect that their employing organization will provide good risk assessment, safety and evacuation procedures. Similarly they expect that their own moral integrity will not compromised while following the mission statement of their organization and to receive psychological and physical follow up for societal reintegration on return through inclusive management of themselves and their families (Busuttil & Busuttil, 2001).

The younger a person is when they contribute to war or disaster the more likely that the experiences will be a critical disruption to early adult development (Elder, 1986; Elder, Shanahan & Clipp, 1995; Pilgrim, Rogers & Bentall, 2009), further complicating any chronic stress reactions, social adjustment and intimate relationship difficulties on return home (McCormack, 2009; McCormack, et al, 2009). Environments that inherently risk safety will induce both biological and cognitive responses to threat impacting on long term psychological adjustment and well-being (Bryant, 2006). Conversely, where safety is prioritised, coping will be enhanced (Solomon & Benbenishty, 1986; Solomon, Shklar & Mikulincer, 2005). With this in mind, the social and psychological consequences of working in warzones including successful post mission reintegration and adjustment, places a duty of care on governments, military caretakers and non-government aid organizations.

Returning from war and disaster environment presents many challenges for reintegration with families, societies and communities. When family, friends and society show little interest, returnees may retreat into their shame in a "conspiracy of silence" fearful of misunderstanding and judgment (Danieli, 1996, Danieli, Stamatopoulou & Dias 1999; Eriksson, Vande Kemp & Gorsuch et al., 2001; McFarlane, 2003a). Unfortunately, disengaging from mission role identity be it civilian or military, and reintegrating with society and family is not uniformly and often poorly addressed by those responsible for the aftercare of disrupted young lives.

The impact of catastrophic events has been described as a shattering of previously held assumptions or an existential blow (Brom & Kelber, 1989; Janoff-Bulman, 1989; 1992). As a result, negative world views may replace previous assumptions which though distressing, can provide a sense of control and rationale over traumatic events. One negative option for making sense of such events and providing explanation is to blame the self (Lerner & Miller, 1978; Lerner, 1980; Littleton, Axson, Radecki Breitkapf & Berenson, 2006; Littleton & Radecki Breitkopf, 2006). Unfortunately, in blaming the self, individuals may experience feelings of guilt or shame. If an individual thinks they have failed to meet personal standards or that they are a bad person, they experience feelings of shame, whereas those who think their actions have harmed others, or feel bad about something they have done, feel guilt (Niedenthal, Tangney & Gavanski, 1994; Tangney & Dearing, 2002). Shame looks inwards on self and distances the individual from their social environment whereas guilt judges the action and motivates the individual towards actions of reparation (Arndt & Goldenberg, 2004; Barrett, 1995; Gramzow & Tangney, 1992; Hall, 1992; Leith & Baumeister, 1998; Tangney, Wagner, Hill-Barlow et al., 1996b). Additionally, guilt and shame may facilitate rejection, disapproval or disinterest from others, can lower self esteem and are predictors of avoidance coping (Dickerson, Gruenewald & Kemeny, 2004; Keltner & Beer, 2005; Leary & Downs, 1995; Leary, Cottrell & Phillips, 2001; Littleton et al, 2006).

Individually, psychological responses to feelings of guilt and shame impact differentially on behavior. Feelings of guilt are more likely to predict other-focused empathy and self-reflection (Joireman, 2004). However with shame, a reciprocal cycle between self-rumination and feelings of shame result in self-focused empathy and personal distress evoking avoidance behaviors, less empathy, displaced anger, and humiliation (Lewis, 1971). Should a chronic sense of having failed personal standards persist, self-destructive, and high risk behaviours may develop (Joireman, 2004; Leith & Baumeister, 1998; Tangney, 1991; Wilson, 2005). Furthermore, shameful rumination, is likely to predict persistent traumatic memories and posttraumatic stress reactions particularly when intense fear, helplessness and horror at the time of the trauma were present (Brewin, Andrew & Rose, 2000; Foa, Steketee & Rothbaum,1989; Pitman, 1997). Wurmser (1987) describes the inner sense of identity being destroyed and 'in danger of symbolically dying' (p. 90) as the result of shame which can lead individuals to narcissistic defenses as a way of protecting fragility or now negatively changed beliefs about themselves.

Individual memories are not independent phenomena but are influenced by the public narrative as it changes over time (Hunt & McHale, 2008). Meaning making is vital to the pursuit of psychological wellbeing and fulfillment of one's potential (Ryan & Deci, 2001; Ryff, 1989). Therefore, entwining personal and public narrative aids reconciliation of traumatic memories by giving a collective meaning to those events (Joseph, Williams, & Yule, 1993; Joseph & Linley, 2005).

However, for trauma-related information to be successfully integrated and comprehensible at a personal level, an individual has to make sense of threatening events and find personal significance for them in their current life (Janoff-Bulman & Franz, 1997; Joseph & Linley, 2005). This necessitates that the independent dimensions of both positive and negative assessment of war are acknowledged if growthful adaptation is to occur (Aldwin, Levenson & Spiro, 1994; Fontana & Rosenheck, 1998; Schok, Kelber, Elands & Weerts, 2008; Spiro, Schnurr & Aldwin, 1999). Military personnel, peacekeepers and veterans have reported an array of positive outcomes and personal growth from war experiences which appear to have mitigated negative consequences and post trauma stress (Aldwin et al.,1994; Britt, Adler & Bartone, 2001; Dohrenwend, Neria &Turner, et al., 2004; Fontana & Rosenheck, 1998; Spiro et al.,1999). In particular, gratitude of society has been recognised as a contributing factor in male veterans coming to terms with their participation in war both in the immediate period after homecoming and 50 or more years after war (Burnell, Coleman & Hunt, 2006; Hautamäki & Coleman, 2001).

Trauma As A Facilitator Of Growth

Conversely we know that stressful and traumatic experiences leading to life threat, uncontrollability and helplessness tend to precipitate growth and that growth inevitably happens when the social environment facilitates self actualization (Joseph & Linley, 2005). However, a question that arises is whether psychological growth is still possible if the social environment is ambivalent and even antagonistic. One of the main facets of growth described by Joseph and Linley (2005) is an individual's ability to change their personal view of themselves that promotes greater resilience, wisdom, and strength as well as accommodation of limitations and vulnerabilities. Through positive reinterpretation of one's actions, acceptance of self and effortful rumination to resolve guilt and shame following exposure to war, genocide, or disaster, positive psychological well-being and psychological growth may occur.

Accordingly, several theories of psychological wellbeing and growth following adversity have developed that elucidate a complex interplay between psychological, social and cultural factors (Joseph & Linley, 2005; Maslow, 1968; Tedeschi & Calhoun, 1995; Rogers, 1963; Ryan & Deci, 2000; Ryff, 1989; Sherman & Cohen, 2006; Steele, 1988). They explain the potential for transformative changes following adversity over-arching three broad life domains: positive re-evaluation of self worth, greater appreciation of interpersonal relationships, changed life values and beliefs (see Joseph & Linley, 2008). For the purpose of this paper, growth refers to psychological wellbeing rather than subjective wellbeing. It is concerned with meaning, schemas, and relationships in contrast to positive affect or life satisfaction which are recognized aspects of subjective wellbeing.

Growth following adversity is not the absence of posttraumatic stress but the ability to consciously and positively redefine world views and self identity following the shattering of core values (Janoff-Bulman, 1989). Considered from a psychosocial framework, distress and growth can be seen as collaborators for posttraumatic adjustment (Joseph & Williams, 2005) promoting eudaimonic psychological wellbeing rather than the immediacy of subjective wellbeing (Helgeson, Reynolds & Tomich, 2006; Joseph & Linley, 2008; Ryff, 1989; Tedeschi & Calhoun, 1995, 2004).

Modern theories of self actualization, self affirmation, psychological wellbeing, and growth are closely aligned to the values encouraged by humility and gratitude (Joseph & Linley, 2005; Tedeschi & Calhoun, 1995; Rogers, 1963; Ryan & Deci, 2000; Ryff, 1989; Sherman & Cohen, 2006; Steele, 1988). Bernard of Clairvaux in the 12th Century (Burch, 1940) described humility as engendering mercy through observing one's own wretchedness and learning to love that weakness in a sad rather than joyous manner. Thus sympathy and love would be extended to others in reciprocal altruism and autonomous self respect. Similarly, Buddhist thinking values humility as a virtue for honest self-assessment (Heim, 2009). This viewpoint regards humility not as low self esteem but truthful self appraisal (Andre, 2002). Having a low opinion of oneself may simply reflect a realistic, honest evaluation of skills while at the same time maintain good self esteem. In other words, it encourages compassion to self, promotes greater resilience, wisdom and personal growth while accommodating limitations and vulnerabilities.

Pre-Christian Aristotelian philosophy aligned eudaimonic happiness or wellbeing with virtuously living in accordance with true self while hubris, thinking too highly of oneself, was considered a vice (McLeod-Harrison, 2005). As such humility leads to sincere and fair interpretation of one's potential and place in the world while aiming for human perfection by thinking no more highly of oneself than is justifiable.

Likewise, gratitude, a personal trait that values and appreciates the positive in life, is strongly related to many aspects of psychological wellbeing and appears to lower levels of stress and depression over time (Wood, Joseph & Maltby, 2009; Wood, Maltby, Gillett, Linley & Joseph, 2008). Rather than focusing on momentary hedonistic pleasure, gratitude appears to promote personal growth through motivation, daily self-regard and the pursuit of social activities that are constructive, satisfying and rewarding (Kashdan, Uswatte & Julian, 2006; Wood, Joseph & Maltby, 2009). When received from society, it can mitigate negative consequences and posttraumatic stress responses after war (Burnell, Coleman & Hunt, 2006; Hautamäki & Coleman, 2001).

Vicarious Debilitation or Vicarious Growth

Working with individuals suffering the extreme consequences and often narcissistic defenses of war shame and grief may personally challenge the therapist. It requires great sensitivity and personal commitment and is not without risk of emotional fatigue, transference and counter-transference for the therapist (Figley, 1995; Wurmser, 1987; Wilson & Thomas, 2004). This phenomenon is variously known as compassion fatigue, secondary traumatic stress and vicarious trauma with transmission appearing to be linked to the carers' susceptibility to emotional contagion followed by emotional distancing in response to feeling overwhelmed (Figley, 1995; 1998; 2005).

To date, there are few studies highlighting growth following secondary traumatization. From the small body of research that does exist evidence for vicarious posttraumatic growth has been conducted with disaster workers, therapists, or families of cancer patients with only one study focusing on both distress and growth in wives of prisoners of war (Dekel, 2007). For example, exposure to disaster relief work in emergency workers produced feelings of wellbeing (Paton, 1996) while firefighters reported an increased appreciation of life and colleagues, and greater sense of control over the unexpected (Moran & Colless, 1995). Following a major train disaster, relief workers reported a causal effect between their disaster work and positive views of their own lives (Raphael, Singh, Bradbury & Lambert, 1983). A small number of studies considering vicarious growth were conducted among family members of patients with cancer. Husbands of wives recovering from cancer reported posttraumatic growth and positive benefits (Manne, Ostroffe, Winkel et al., 2004; Weiss, 2004) as did the parents of adolescents survivors of cancer, and the adolescents (Barakat, Alderfer, & Kazak, 2005). In recognition of the potential cost to working as therapists in the field of trauma, one study found that a greater sense of coherence was associated with fewer negative changes and more positive changes (Linley, Joseph & Loumidis, 2005). Similarly, Shiri et al (2008) found that Israeli doctors, nurses and psychotherapists treating victims of politically motivated violence reported positive changes in perceptions of relationships.

A Phenomenological Interpretation for Good Practice

Understanding the dynamics for growthful adaptation following war or combat distress is an important endeavor for the future and needs the dual insights of epistemological and phenomenological analysis alongside that of cause and effect. Given the ad hoc and labile political objectives that often engage young soldiers in spurious wars, it is likely that partners and families will continue to provide the major resources in post war care supported by therapists who themselves can be challenged by the work. Currently, political and economic support is based on a medical model of interpretation that isolates the individual as the problem exonerating any role played by society in questionable wars.

Political and economic climates since the growth of the Diagnostic and Statistical Manual of Mental Disorders (APA:DSM; 1980; 1987;1994; 2000) have focused on an individual mental illness paradigm of combat and war trauma that reverberates with an individual therapeutic narrative rather than the collective narrative that brings healing to a community (Bloom,

1998). However, adopting a therapeutic personal narrative can further contribute to the abdication of societal conscience and further victimize the individual. As such the positivist view traditionally adhered to for so called evidence-based guidance relies on a mental ill health paradigm and medical model to explain human suffering.

This alliance and specialization approach has seduced practitioners/researchers to 'expertly' label and categorize human experience rather than collaboratively investigate with the client how they bring meaning to their experiences. What is obvious is that there has been an absence of curiosity into other etiologies of mental distress particularly traumatic events, in preference for the clinical trials of treatment response, and pharmaceuticals dispensed (Perez-Alvarez, Sass & Garcia-Montes, 2009). Following the involvement in war by any society, framing subjective distress with cultural and historical understanding rather than labeling an individual as the problem (Maddox, Snyder & Lopez, 2004), provides a platform for democratic inclusiveness that is reparative, informative and therapeutic for both the individual and society. The humility and wisdom to take off the hat of the expert and stay open to the unique perspective of rebuilding a life shattered by complex traumatic events recognizes the limitation of a one method panacea.

A phenomenological approach to psychological suffering on the other hand reflexively suspends presuppositions and considers the subjective experience within cultural contexts. It is exploratory and iterative looking to build an inclusive narrative between the individual and society. It is well known that the social environment can offer the nurturance necessary for veterans to adjust from traumatic combat experiences (Jones, 1953; Bloom, 1997) especially when egalitarian, honest, open and trusting interactions prevail (Almond, 1974; Rapoport, 1960). Collective generalizations or causes and effects of quantitative research tell us a great deal about populations however, subjective consideration that looks for uniqueness gives insights into psychological phenomena that are invisible to a quantitative approach. Phenomenological enquiry requires a very different mindset—there are no generalizable outcomes across a population, nor are there right or wrong answers or cause and effect conclusions to be made. It does not dispute physical reality as separate from our conscious experience of it. It is the individual's interpretation of their reality in time and place that is sought.

Summary

The sense of loss that accompanies perceived moral failure can inhibit the construction of meshed stories through dialogue that bring meaning to events (Harvey, 2002). Without the acceptance of intimate others and colleagues, and an opportunity for their stories to be incorporated in the public narrative, the private narrative may remain self blaming for many years as many veterans and their families found following the Vietnam War. However, organizations who extend reintegration protocols post mission to include families/intimate others, as a consequence may affect better outcomes in the field and staff retention. Understandably, addressing the humanitarian protocols: sense of belonging, sense of control, social support, meaningfulness and human dignity; which are equally valid for the carer as for the recipient of care, a post mission protocol for reintegration and rehabilitation could include the following: 'debriefing' and psychological assessment; psychosocial rehabilitation with family, community and workplace; and psycho-educational sessions for both aid worker and family members (McCormack et al, 2009).

First, the specific cognitive-emotive-cognitive debriefing regime of Critical Incident Stress Management (CISM) (Mitchell,1983; Everly & Mitchell, 2000) for validating yet calming following traumatic distress, can provide a springboard for those few individuals needing further intervention. However, it is important to clarify it was not designed as a psychotherapeutic intervention for traumatized individuals. It is designed for follow ups and primarily for use with secondary victims, hence appropriate in many instances for aid workers and other support personnel (Dyregrov, 1989; 1998).

However, second, this should not stand alone but be incorporated with 'psychosocial' support from practice based research and 'lessons-learned' in the field (Berliner & Regel, 2008). Such programs were developed to place shattered communities centre stage in re-establishing their sense of place (Prewitt Diaz & Dayal, 2008) and as mentioned can work equally well with the carers and their extended support family on return. They are designed to orient the individual after catastrophic events towards personal growth by facilitating their focus on redefining their place in the world, prioritizing listening and understanding before action, and collaboratively identifying knowledge of support networks. Potentially such protocols for social reintegration on returning home could be incorporated into post mission clearance procedures.

A third component, psycho-educational support encompasses a wealth of strategies and skills for aiding psychological adjustment. These psycho-educational tools enhance problem solving, normalize responses, and empower individuals and families in empathic listening and self care as they reintegrate and transcend the dissociative experiences of homecoming. One model that is similar to this has been developed over the last 20 years to assist Australian veterans and their families. Through the initiative of Vietnam veterans a free counseling service for veterans and their families is nationwide supported but separate from the positivist model for remuneration administered by the Department of Veterans Affairs.

It is well to remember that debriefing has met with controversy (Almedon & Summerfield, 2004; Bracken, 2002; Devilly & Cotton, 2003; Dyregrov, 1998; Everly, 2003; Hobfoll, Watson & Bell et al., 2007; Pupavac, 2004; Regel, Dyregrov & Joseph, 2007; Rose, Bisson, & Wessely, 2002; Wagner, 2005; Weseley, Rose & Bisson, 1999). As such the use of debriefing should be incorporated with psychosocial and psycho-educational support. As part of a package of post mission support debriefing offers the beginning of adjustment and validation from deployment organizations. But social disruption and mental health problems are more complex issues post mission and as such are likely to require more holistic and ongoing contact to ensure healthy reintegration.

Cross-cultural research offers specific challenges for the researcher. However, a phenomenological approach to unraveling storytelling and narratives also validates the individual's right to redefine their own futures and make sense of experiences whatever their cultural background. It philosophically underpins many psychosocial programs in disaster response and is used to trigger adaptive processes and psychological growth. Used inclusively and respectfully, such programs facilitate positive change, future goals and a commonality of communication across all cultures (McCormack, in press).

In conclusion, a phenomenological reflective and reiterative approach to the experiences of others, irrespective of cultural background can facilitate and support respectful self determination and contribute towards societal inclusiveness. Working from a medical model, be it as a therapist assisting meaning making following complex international events or on an international humanitarian mission supporting communities in distress, risks medicalization of others' experiences. However a phenomenological perspective allows the individual to honestly self examine using their own resources and energy to redefine their experiences. In providing an environment for self determination, self reparation and psychological growth, the therapist or support personnel may vicariously experience self awareness and positive change in their own perceptions. Although psychiatric expertise is invaluable in the treatment of psychiatric distress and can benefit veteran tribunals, insurance companies, law courts, and police, the trauma therapist and disaster interventionist must be aware that labeling with psychiatric diagnoses, may contribute to a further sense of betrayal and alienation in those struggling to make sense of their shattered values and purpose. By standing beside our clients and communities in need, and bracketing out our own biases and preconceptions, there is less chance that a power imbalance will occur that inhibits growthful self examination. Honoring and validating empathically the individual's ability to make sense of their experiences can bring hope for their future and restoration of the altruistic identity of those involved in complex international conflicts.

About the Author

Lynne McCormack has worked as a health, educational, clinical and trauma psychologist for over 20 years but tends to regard herself as a social psychologist viewing her clients as the experts in their own lives. She has managed her own private practice, and consulted in hospitals, schools and emergency services. During that time she has come to recognize that although many individuals suffer extreme psychological distress following traumatic events many were able to redefine their lives positively. Lynne's interest in both positive and negative human response to extremely traumatic environment grew from her own involvement in the Vietnam war. Her postgraduate research areas are civilian women in war and the subjective phenomenological interpretations of experiencing disaster, war and genocide.

Lynne has worked widely with those exposed to traumatic incidents including military veterans and their families, aid workers, and civilians re-adjusting to the long term consequences of war, tragic death, health and other personal trauma. During much of that time she has been on call for critical incidents and as an advocate for children at risk. From an earlier life career as a music teacher Lynne has come to appreciate the many ways in which individuals' resource their own talents and skills for recovery. She has been part of training workshops following critical incident, chronic pain, relationship challenges, abuse, and post war distress incorporating individual creativity for mental wellbeing. Apart from her time in Vietnam she has worked in humanitarian aid designing, developing and evaluating health and psychosocial programs in East Timor post war, and Aceh following the Tsunami. Lynne recognizes individuals as the expert in their own lives however, as desired by her clients, is trained in EMDR, CBT and CISM. Like many, Lynne loves to travel and has worked and lived for many years in Southeast Asia, the Pacific, Australia and the UK.

Correspondence to:
Lynne McCormack
Trauma Psychologist

Centre for Trauma, Resilience and Growth (CTRG)
School of Sociology and Social Policy
University of Nottingham
Nottingham NG7 2RD UK
+44 (0) 7726108984
Email: creativepsych@gmail.com or lqxlm2@nottingham.ac.uk

References

Aldwin, C. M., Levenson, M. R., & Spiro, A. (1994). Vulnerability and resilience to combat exposure: can stress have lifelong effects? Psychology and Aging, 1, 34–44.

Almedom, A & Summerfield, D. (2004). Mental well-being in settings of 'complex emergency': An overview. *Journal of Biosocial Sciences*, 36, 381-388.

Almond, R. *The healing community*. New York: Jason Aronson, Inc., 1974.

American Psychiatric Association. (1980). *Diagnostic and statistical manual of mental disorders* (3rd ed.). Washington, DC: Author.

American Psychiatric Association. (1987*). Diagnostic and statistical manual of mental disorders* (3rd ed. rev.). Washington, DC: Author.

American Psychiatric Association. (1994). *Diagnostic and statistical manual of mental disorders* (4th ed.). Washington, DC: Author.

American Psychiatric Association. (2000). *Diagnostic and statistical manual of mental disorders* (4th ed.TR). Washington, DC: Author.

Andre, J. (2002). Humility. In: H. La Follette (Eds.), *Ethics in practice*. 276-284. Oxford: Blackwell Publishing.

Arndt, J. & Goldenberg, J. K. (2004). From self-awareness to shame-proneness: evidence of causal sequence among women. Self Identity, 3, 27-37.

Arnold, D., Calhoun, L., Tedeschi, R. & Cann, A. (2005). Vicarious posttraumatic growth in psychotherapy. Journal of Humanistic Psychology, 45, 2, 239-263.

Ashton, M. C., & Lee, K. (2008). The prediction of honesty-humility-related criteria by the HEXACO and five-factor models of personality. Journal of Research in Personality, 42, 1216-1228.

Barakat, L., Alderfer, M & Kazak, A. (2005). Posttraumatic Growth in Adolescent Survivors of Cancer and Their Mothers and Fathers Barnett, M (2005). Humanitarianism Transformed. Perspectives on Politics, 3, 4, 723-740.

Barrett, K. C. (1995). A Functionalist Approach to Shame and Guilt. In: Self-Conscious Emotions. Ed. J. P. Tangney & K. W. Fischer, (pp. 25-63). Guildford Press: New York.

Berliner, P., & Regel, S. (2008). Essential elements of mass trauma intervention. Coping With Crisis Newsletter, 2, 12.

Blanchetiere, P. (2006). Resilience of humanitarian workers. Retrieved February 8, 2008, from: http://www.peopleinaid.org.uk/pool/files/publications/resilience-of-aid-workers-article.pdf

Bloom, S. L. (1997). Creating Sanctuary: Toward the Evolution of Sane societies. New York, NY: Routledge.

Bowlby, J. (1960). Separation anxiety. International journal of Psychoanalysis, 41, 89-113.

Bracken, P. (2002). Trauma: Culture, Meaning and Philosophy. London: Whurr.

Brady, J. L., Guy, J. D., Poelstra, P. L. & Brokaw, B. F. (1999). Vicarious traumatisation, spirituality, and the treatment o sexual abuse survivors: A national survey of women psychotherapists. Professional Psychology: Research and Practice, 30, 386-393.

Brewin, C. R., Andrews, B. & Rose, S. (2000). Fear, helplessness and horror in posttraumatic stress disorder: Investigating DSM-IV criterion A2 in victims of violent crime. Journal of Traumatic Stress, 13, 499-509.

Brewin, C. R., Dalgleish, T., & Joseph, S. (1996). A dual representation theory of posttraumatic stress disorder. Psychological Review, 103, 670–686.

Britt, T.W., Adler, A. B., & Bartone, P. T. (2001). Deriving benefits from stressful events: The role of engagement in meaningful work and hardiness. Journal of Occupational Health Psychology, 1, 53–63.

Brom, D. & Kleber, R. J. (1989). Prevention of post-traumatic stress disorders. Journal of Traumatic Stress, 2, 335-349.

Bryant, R. (2006). Acute stress disorder. Psychiatry, 5, 7, 238-239.

Burch, G. B., trans. (1940). Bernard of Clairvaux's the steps of humility. Cambridge: Harvard University Press.

Burnell, K. J., Coleman, P. G., & Hunt, N. (2006). Falklands War veterans' perceptions of social support and the reconciliation of traumatic memories. Aging and Mental Health, 10, 282-289.

Busuttil, W. & Busuttil, A. (2001). Psychological effects on families subjected to enforced and prolonged separations generated under life threatening situations. Sexual and Relationship Therapy, 16, 3. 207-228.

Calhoun, L. G., & Tedeschi, R. G. (1998). Beyond recovery from trauma: Implications for clinical practice and research. Journal of Social Issues, 54, 357-371.

Camp, N. M. (1993). The Vietnam war and the ethics of combat psychiatry. American Journal of Psychiatry, 150, 7, 1000-1010.

Chandler, D. (2009). War without end(s): Grounding the discourse of 'Global War'.

Danieli, Y. (1996) 'Confronting the Unimaginable: Psychotherapists' Reactions to Victims of the Nazi Holocaust'. In J. P. Wilson, Z. Harek, and B. Kahana (Eds.) Human Adaptation to Extreme Stress: From the Holocaust to Vietnam (Pp. 219-238). Plenum Press, New York.

Danieli, Y., Stamatopoulou, E. & Dias, D. J. (Eds.). (1999). *The universal declaration of human rights: Fifty years and beyond.* Amityville, NY: Baywood.

Dekel, R. (2007). Posttraumatic distress and growth among wives of prisoners of war: The contribution of husbands' posttraumatic stress disorder and wives' own attachment. American journal of Orthopsychiatry, 77, 3, 419-426

Dekel, R. & Solomon, Z. (2006). Secondary traumatization among wives of Israeli POWs: the role of POWs' distress. Social Psychiatry and Psychiatric Epidemiology, 41, 27-33.

De Prince, A. P., & Freyd, J. J. (2002). The harm of trauma: pathological fear, shattered assumptions or betrayal? In J. Kauffman (Ed.). Loss of the Assumptive World: a theory of traumatic loss. Pp 71-82. New York: .Brunner-Routledge.

Hobfoll, S. E., Watson, P., Bell, C. C., Bryant, R. A., Brymer, M. J., Friedman, M. J., et al. (2007). Five essential elements of immediate and mid-term mass trauma intervention: Empirical evidence. Psychiatry, 70, 283-315.

Devilly, G. J., & Cotton, P. (2003). Psychological debriefing and the workplace: Defining a concept, controversies and guidelines for intervention. Australian Psychologist, 38, 144-150.

Dickerson, S. S.; Gruenewald, T. L. & Kemeny, M. E. (2004). When the social self is threatened: shame, physiology and health. Journal of Personality, 72, 1189-1216.

Dohrenwend, B. P., Neria, Y., Turner, J. B., Turse, N., Marshall, R., Lewis-Fernandez, R., et al. (2004). Positive tertiary appraisals and post-traumatic stress disorder in U.S. male veterans of the war in Vietnam: the roles of positive affirmation, positive reformulation, and defensive denial. Journal of Consulting and Clinical Psychology, 3, 417–433.

Doka, K. J. (2002). Disenfranchised grief: New Direction, challenges, and strategies for practice. USA: Malloy Lithographing, Inc.

Dyregrov, A. (1989). Caring for helpers in disaster situations: Psychological debriefing. Disaster Management, 2, 25-30.

Dyregrov, A. (1998). Psychological debriefing: An effective method? Traumatology, 4, 6-15.

Elder, G. H. (1986). Military times and turning points in men's lives. Developmental Psychology, 22, 233-245.

Elder, G.H., Shanahan, M.J., & Clipp, E.C. (1995). Linking combat and physical health: The legacy of World War II in men's lives. American Journal of Psychiatry, 154, 330-336.

Eriksson, C. B., Vande Kemp, H., Gorsuch, R., Hoke, S., & Foy, D. W. (2001). Trauma exposure and PTSD symptoms in international relief and development personnel. Journal of Traumatic Stress, 14, 205-212.

Everly, G. S. (2003). Early psychological intervention: A word of caution. International Journal of Emergency Mental Health, 5, 179-183.

Everly, G. S., Jr., & Mitchell, J. T. (2000). The debriefing "controversy" and crisis intervention: A review of lexical and substantive issues. International Journal of Emergency Mental Health, 2, 211-225.

Fawcett, J. (2004). Preventing broken hearts, healing broken minds. In D. Yael (Ed.), Sharing the front line and the back hills. International protectors and providers: Peacekeepers, humanitarian aid workers and the media in the midst of crisis. Amityville, NY: Baywood, (pp. 223-235).

Fiala, A. (2008). The just war myth. New York: Rowman & Littlefield Publishers, Inc.

Figley, C. R. (2005). Strangers at home: Comment on Dirkswager, Bramsen, Ader and van der Ploeg (2005). Journal of Family Psychology, 19, 227-229.

Figley, C. R. (Ed). (1998). Burnout in Families: The Systemic Costs of Caring. Boca Raton: CRS Press.

Figley, C. R. (Ed.). (1995). Compassion Fatigue. Coping with secondary traumatic stress disorder in those who treat the traumatized. Florence: Brunner/Mazel.

Foa, E. B., Steketee, G. & Rothbaum, B. O. (1989). Behavioural/cognitive conceptualizations of post-traumatic stress disorder. Behavioural Therapist, 20, 155-176.

Fontana, A., & Rosenheck, R. (1998). Psychological benefits and liabilities of traumatic exposure in the war zone. Journal of Traumatic Stress, 3, 485–503.

Freud, S. (1917). Mourning and melancholia. In: Sigmund Freud collected papers , 4, 152-173. New York: Basic Books.

Freyd, J. J. (1996). The Logic of Forgetting Childhood Abuse. Betrayal Trauma. London: Harvard University Press

Gaines, R. (1997). Detachment and continuity: The two tasks of mourning. Contemporary Psychoanalysis, 33, 4, 549–571.

Grant, R. (1995). Trauma in missionary life. Missiology, 23, 71-83.

Gilbert, P. (2004). Evolution, attractiveness, and the emergence of shame and guilt in a self-aware mind: A reflection on Tracy and Robins. Psychological Inquiry, 15, 132-135.

Gramzow, R. H. & Tangney, J. P. (1992). Proneness to shame and the narcissistic personality. Personality and Social Psychological Bulletin, 18, 369-376.

Hagman, G. (2001). Beyond decathexis: toward a new psychoanalytic understanding and treatment of mourning. In Neimeyer, R. (Ed.), Meaning reconstruction and the experience of loss (pp.13-32). Washington, DC: American Psychological Association.

Hall, J. A. (1992). Psychological-mindedness: A conceptual model. American Journal of Psychotherapy, 46, 131-140.

Harvey, J. H. (2002). Perspectives of loss and trauma. Assaults on the self. California: Sage Publications.

Hautamäki, A. & Coleman, P. G. (2001). Explanation for low prevalence of PTSD among older Finnish war veterans: Social solidarity and continued significance given to wartime sufferings. Aging and Mental Health, 5, 165-174.

Heim, M. (2009). The conceit of self-loathing. Journal of Indian Philosophy, 37, 61-74.

Helgeson, V. S., Reynolds, K. A. & Tomich, P. L. (2006). A meta-analytic review of benefit finding and growth. Journal of Consulting and Clinical psychology, 74. 5, 797-816.

Hobfoll, S. E., Watson, P., Bell, C. C., Bryant, R. A., Brymer, M. J., Friedman, M. J., et al. (2007). Five essential elements of immediate and mid-term mass trauma intervention: Empirical evidence. Psychiatry, 70, 283-315.

Hogan, N. S. & Schmidt, L. A. (2002). Testing the grief to personal growth model using structural equation modelling. Death Studies, 26, 615-634.

Hunt, N. & McHale, S. (2008). Memory and meaning: Individual and social aspects of memory narratives. Journal of Loss and Trauma. 13. 1. 42-58.

Hynes, H. P. (2004). On the battlefield of women's bodies: An overview of the harm of war to women. Women's Studies International Forum, 27, 431-445.

Janoff-Bulman, R. (1989). Assumptive worlds and the stress of traumatic events: Applications of the schema construct. Social Cognition, 7, 113-136.

Janoff-Bulman, R. (1992). Shattered Assumptions: Towards a new psychology of trauma. New York: The Free Press.

Janoff-Bulman, R., & Frantz, C. M. (1997). The impact of trauma on meaning: From meaningless world to meaningful live. In M. Power & C.R.Brewin (Eds.). The transformation of meaning in psychological therapies (pp. 91–106). Chichester, England: Wiley.

Joireman, J. (2004). Empathy and the self-absorption paradox II: Self-rumination and self-reflection as mediators between shame, guilt and empathy. Self and Identity, 3. 225-238.

Jones, M. (1953). *The therapeutic community*. New York: Basic Books.

Joseph, S., & Linley, P. (2005). Positive adjustment to threatening events: An organismic valuing theory of growth through adversity. Review of General Psychology, 9, 262-280.

Joseph, S. & Linley, P. (Eds.). (2008). Trauma, recovery and growth. Positive psychological perspectives on posttraumatic stress. New Jersey: John Wiley & Sons.

Joseph. S. & Williams, R. (2005). Understanding posttraumatic stress: theory, reflections, context and future. Behavioural and Cognitive Psychotherapy, 33, 423-441.

Joseph, S., Williams. R. & Yule. W. (1993). Changes in outlook following disaster: The preliminary development of a measure to assess positive and negative response. Journal of Traumatic Stress. 6. 271-279.

Kashdan, T. B., Uswatte, G. & Julian, T. (2006). Gratitude and hedonic and eudaimonic wellbeing in Vietnam War veterans. Behaviour Research and Therapy, 44, 177-199.

Kaufman, G. (2002). Safety and the assumptive world. In: J. Kauffman (Ed.). Loss of the assumptive world. New York: Brunner-Routledge.

Kaur, M. (1996). *Who helps the helper: Analysis of management of stress and trauma in humanitarian aid workers in complex emergencies*. Unpublished master's thesis, Queen Margaret College, Edinburgh.

Keltner, D. & Beer, J. S. (2005). Self-conscious emotion and self-regulation. In On Building, Defending, and Regulating the Self: A Psychological Perspective. Ed. A. Tesser, J. V. Wood, D. A. Stapel. Pp. 197-215. New York: Psychology Press.

Kübler-Ross, E. (1982). *Working it through*. New York: Macmillan.

Leary, M. R. & Downs, D. L. (1995). Interpersonal functions of the self-esteem motive: the self-esteem system as a sociometer. In Efficacy, Agency and Self-Esteem. Ed. M. Kernis, (pp.123-144). New York: Plenum.

Leary, M. R., Cottrell, C. A. & Phillips, M. (2001). Deconfounding the effects of dominance and social acceptance on self-esteem. Journal of Personality and Social Psychology, 81, 898-909.

Leith, K. P. & Baumeister, R. F. (1998). Empathy, shame, guilt, and narratives of interpersonal conflicts: Guilt-prone people are better at perspective taking. Journal of Personality, 66, 1-37.

Lerner, M. J. (1980). The Belief in a Just World: A Fundamental Delusion, New York: Plenum Press.

Lerner, M. J. & Miller, D. T. (1978). Just world research and the attribution process: Looking back and ahead. Psychological Bulletin, 85, 1030-1051.

Lewis, H. B. (1971). Shame and Guilt in Neurosis. New York: International University Press.

Linley, P. Alex, Joseph, S. & Loumidis, K. (2005). Trauma work, sense of coherence, and positive and negative changes in therapists. Psychotherapy and Psychosomatics, 74, 185-188.

Littleton, H. & Radecki Breitkopf, C. (2006). Coping with the experience of rape. Psychology of Women Quarterly, 30, 106-116.

Littleton, H. L., Axsom, D., Radecki Breitkopf, C. & Berenson, A. (2006). Rape acknowledgement and post assault experiences: How acknowledgement status relates to disclosure, coping, worldview, and reactions received from others. Violence and Victims, 21, 761-778.

Loquercio, D. (2006). Turnover and retention. Retrieved January 3, 2008, from http://www.peopleinaid.org/pool/ files/publications/turnover-and-retention-lit-review-jan- 2006.pdf

Macnair, R. (1995). Room for Improvement: The management and support of relief and development workers. London: Overseas Development Institute.

Maddux, J. E., Snyder, C. R., & Lopez, S. J. (2004). Towards a positive clinical psychology: Deconstructing the illness ideology and constructing an ideology of human strengths and potential. In P. A. Linley & Joseph (Eds.). Positive psychology in practice. Pp. 320-334). Hoboken, NJ: Wiley.

Manne, S., Ostroff, J., Winkel, G., Goldstein, L., Fox, K., & Grana, G. (2004). Posttraumatic growth after breast cancer: Patient, partner and couple perspectives. Psychosomatic Medicine, 66, 442–454.

Maslow, A. H. (1968) *Towards a psychology of being* (2nd Ed.). New York: Van Nostrand.

McCall, M., & Salama, P. (1999). Training and support of relief workers: An occupational health issue. British Medical Journal, 318, 113-116.

McCormack, L. (in press, 2010). Most Significant Change Technique: The value of storytelling cross-culturally in assessing psychosocial programmes. Qualitative Methods in Psychological Research.

McCormack, L. (2009). Civilian women at war: Psychological impact decades after the Vietnam. Journal of Loss and Trauma. 14, 447-458.

McCormack, L., Joseph, S. & Hagger, M. S. (2009). Sustaining a positive altruistic identity in humanitarian aid work: A qualitative case study. Traumatology. 15, 2, 109-118.

McFarlane, C. (2003a). The balance of trauma, stress and resilience by international aid workers: A longitudinal qualitative investigation. Paper presented at the 10th annual conference of the Australasian Society for Traumatic Stress Studies, Hobart, Australia.

McLeod-Harrison, M. (2005). Repairing Eden: Humility, Mysticism, and the Existentialist Problem of Religious Diversity. Montreal, Canada: McGill-Queen's University Press.

Mitchell, J. T. (1983). When disaster strikes: The critical incident stress debriefing process. Journal of Emergency Medical Services, 8, 36-39.

Moran, C. & Colless, E. (1995). Positive reactions following emergency and disaster responses. Disaster Prevention and Management, 4, 55-61.

Niedenthal, P. M. Tangney, J. P. & Gavanski, I. (1994). 'If only I weren't' versus 'if only I hadn't': distinguishing shame and guilt in counterfactual thinking. Journal of Personality and Social Psychology, 67. 585-595.

Parkes, C. M., & Weiss, R. S. (1983). Recovery from bereavement. New York: Basic Books.

Paton, D. (1996). Training disaster workers: promoting well-being and operational effectiveness. Disaster Prevention and Management, 5, 10-16.

Pearlman, L. A. & Saakvitne, K.W. (1995). Trauma and the therapist: Countertransference and vicarious traumatization in psychotherapy with incest survivors. New York: Norton.

Pérez-Álvarez, M., Sass, L. A. & García-Montes, J. M. (2009). More Aristotle, Less DSM: The ontology of mental disorders in constructivist perspective. Philsophy, Psychiatry & Psychology, 15, 3, 211-225.

Pilgrim, D., Rogers, A., & Bentall, R. (2009). The centrality of personal relationships in the creation and amelioration of mental health problems: the current interdisciplinary case. Health 13, 235 – 254.

Pitman, R. K. (1997). Overview of biological themes in PTSD. In: R. Yehuda, A. C. McFarlane (Eds.). Psychobiology of Posttraumatic Stress Disorder, 821. 1-9. NY: New York Academy of Sciences.

Prati, G. & Pietrantoni, L. (2009). Optimism, social support and coping straties as factors contributing to posttraumatic growth: A meta-analysis. Journal of Loss and Trauma, 14. 364-388.

Prewitt Diaz, J. O. & Dayal, A. (2008) Sense of Place: A Model for Community Based Psychosocial Support Programs. The Australasian Journal of Disaster and Trauma Studies, 1. http://www.massey.ac.nz/~trauma/issues/2008-1/prewitt_diaz.htm

Pupavac, V. (2004). Psychosocial interventions and the demoralization of humanitarianism. Journal of Biosocial Science, 36, 491-504.

Raphael B, Singh B, Bradbury L and Lambert F (1983) Who helps the Helper? The effects of disaster on the rescue workers. Omega: Journal of Death and Dying 14, 9-20.

Rapoport, R. N. (1960) *Community as doctor*. London: Tavistock.

Regel, S., Dyregrov, A., & Joseph, S. (2007). Psychological debriefing in cross-cultural contexts: Ten implications for practice. International Journal of Emergency Mental Health, 9, 37-45.

Rogers, C. (1963). The actualising tendency in relation to "motives" and to consciousness. In Nebraska Symposium on Motivation, Ed. M. R. Jones, 11:1-24. Lincoln: University Nebraska Press.

Rose, S., Bisson, J., & Wessely, S. (2002). Psychological debriefing for preventing posttraumatic stress disorder (PTSD). Cochrane Database of Systematic Reviews, 1, CD000560.

Ryan, R. M. & Deci, E. L. (2000). Self-determination theory and the facilitation of intrinsic motivation, social development, and well-being. American Psychologist, 55, 68-78.

Ryan, R. M., & Deci, E. L. (2001). On happiness and human potentials: A review of research on hedonic and eudaimonic well-being. Annual Review of Psychology, 52, 141-166.

Ryff, C. (1989). Happiness is everything, or is it? Explorations on the meaning of psychological well-being. Journal of Personality and Social Psychology. 57, 1069-1081.

Schauben, L. J. & Frazier, P. A. (1995). Vicarious trauma: The effects on female counsellors of working with sexual violence survivors. Psychology of Women Quarterly, 19, 49-64

Schok, M. L., Kleber, R. J., Elands, M. & Weerts, J. M. P. (2008). Meaning as mission: a review of empirical studies on appraisals of war and peacekeeping experiences. Clinical Psychology Review, 28, 357-365.

Schouten, E. J., & Borgdorff, M. W. (1995). Increased mortality among Dutch development workers. British Medical Journal, 311, 1343-1344.

Security Dialogue, 40, 3, 243-262.

Shay, J. (1994). Achilles in Vietnam. Combat trauma and the undoing of character. New York: Scribner.

Sheik, M., Gutierrez, M., Bolton, P. I., Speigel, P., Thieren, M., &. Burnham. G. (2000). Deaths among humanitarian aid workers. British Medical Journal, 231, 166-168.

Sherman, D. K., & Cohen, J. L. (2006). The psychology of self-defense: Self-affirmation theory. In M. P. Zanna (Ed.), Advances in experimental social psychology (Vol. 38, pp. 183-242). San Diego, CA: Academic Press.

Shiri, S., Wexler, I. S., Alkalay, Y., Meiner, Z & Kreitler, S. (2008). Positive psychological impact of treating victims of politically motivated violence among hospital-based health care providers. Psychotherapy and psychosomatics, 77, 315-318.

Solomon, Z. & Benbenishty, R. (1986). The role of proximity, immediacy, and expectancy in frontline treatment of combat stress reaction among Israelis in the Lebanon War. American Journal of Psychiatry, 143, 5, 613-617.

Solomon, Z., Shklar, R. & Milkulincer, M. (2005). Frontline treatment of combat stress reaction: A 20-year longitudinal evaluation study. American Journal of Psychiatry, 162, 2309-2314.

Spiro, A., Schnurr, P. P., & Aldwin, C. M. (1999). A life-span perspective on the effects of military service. Journal of Geriatric Psychiatry, 30, 92–128.

Steele, C. M. (1988). The psychology of self-affirmation: Sustaining the integrity of the self. In L. Berkowitz (Ed.): Advances in experimental social psychology (Vol. 21, pp. 261-302). New York: Academic Press.

Tangney, J. P., (1991). Moral affect: The good, the bad, and the ugly. Journal of personality and Social Psychology, 61, 598-607.

Tangney, J. P., & Dearing, R. L. (2002). Shame and Guilt. New York: Guilford.

Tangney, J. P., Wagner, P. E., Hill-Barlow, D. H., Marschall, D. E. & Gramzow, R.H. (1996b). Relations of shame and guilt to constructive versus destructive responses to anger across the lifespan. Journal of Personality and Social Psychology, 70, 797-809.

Tedeschi, R. G. & Calhoun, L.G. (1995). Trauma and Transformation: Growing in the aftermath of suffering. Thousand Oaks, CA: Sage.

Tedeschi, R.G. & Calhoun, L.G. (1996). The posttraumatic growth inventory: measuring the positive legacy of trauma. Journal of Traumatic Stress, 9, 455-471.

Tedeschi, R. G. & Calhoun, L. G. (2004). Posttraumatic growth: Conceptual foundations and empirical evidence. Psychological Inquiry, 15, 1, 1-18.

Thompson, S. C. & Janigian, A. (1988). Life schemes: A framework for understanding the search for meaning. Journal of Social and Clinical Psychology, 7, 260-280.

Van Vliet, K. J. (2009). The role of attributions in the process of overcoming shame: A qualitative analysis. Psychology and Psychotherapy: Theory, Research and Practice, 82, 137-152.

Veatch, R. M. (1977). Soldier, physician and moral man. In: Case Studies in Medical Ethics. (Ed.): R.M. Veatch. Cambridge Mass: Harvard University Press.

Volkan, V. D., & Zintl, E. (1993). Life after loss. New York: Scribner.

Wagner, S. L. (2005). Emergency response service personnel and the critical incident stress debriefing debate. International Journal of Emergency Mental Health, 7, 33-41.

Walzer, M. (1977). Just and unjust wars: A moral argument with historical illustrations. New York: Basic Books.

Weiner, B. (1995). Judgements of responsibility: A foundation for the theory of social conduct. New York, NY: Guilford.

Weiss, T. (2004). Correlates of posttraumatic growth in married breast cancer survivors. Journal of Social and Clinical Psychology, 23, 733-746.

Weseley, S., Rose, S., & Bisson, J. (1999). Brief Psychological Interventions ('Debriefing') for Immediate Trauma Related Symptoms and the Prevention of Post Traumatic Stress Disorder (Cochrane Review), The Cochrane Library, 4, Update Software, Oxford.

Wilson, J. P. (2005). The posttraumatic self: Restoring meaning and wholeness to personality. New York: Brunner-Routledge.

Wilson, J. P. & Drozdek, B. (2006). Posttraumatic Shame and Guilt. Trauma, Violence & Abuse, 7, 2, 122-141.

Wilson, J. P. & Lindy, J. D. (1994). Empathic strain and countertransference. In J. P. Wilson & J. D. Lindy (Eds.). Countertransference in the treatment of PTSD. Pp. 5-30. New York: Guilford.

Wilson, J. P. & Thomas, R. (2004). Empathy in the treatment of trauma and PTSD. New York: Brunner-Routledge.

Wood, A. M., Joseph, S. & Maltby, J. (2009). Gratitude predicts psychological well-being above the big five facets. Personality and Individual Differences, 46, 443-447.

Wood, A. M., Maltby, J., Gillett, R., Linley, P. A. & Joseph, S. (2008). The role of gratitude in the development of social support, stress, and depression: Two longitudinal studies. Journal of Research in Personality, 42, 854-871.

Wurmser, L. (1987). Shame: The veiled companion of narcissism. In D. L. Nathanson (Ed.). The many faces of shame, (Pp 64-92). New York: Guildford.

Being There When It Counts: Mental Health Roles

George W. Doherty, MS, LPC

President, Rocky Mountain Region Disaster Mental Health Institute

Abstract

Disaster Mental Health has not generally been given priority by emergency preparedness planners. A disaster mental health plan is essential for coordination of mental health emergency response efforts with other emergency response organizations during and following disasters. Each state department of mental health should have a behavioral health/mental health disaster plan which is a component of the state emergency management plan. This plan should also include cultural and ethnic components. This presentation outlines some factors to take into account in developing such a disaster mental health plan and the role of mental health as part of the team in the Emergency Operations Center (EOC).

The Concept of Disaster Mental Health

Anyone who sees a disaster cannot remain untouched by it. Loss and trauma directly affect many people in disasters. There are also many others who are emotionally impacted by simply being a part of the affected community. Seeing massive destruction and other terrible sights evoke deep strong feelings. Residents of communities stricken by disaster often report feelings of grief, sadness, anxiety, and anger even if they themselves are not victims. These strong reactions may confuse them because they, themselves, were spared personal loss. It is important to remember that everyone who sees a disaster is, in some sense, a victim. Even persons who experience a disaster "second hand" through exposure to media coverage can be affected. This includes children whose parents might lose track of how much disaster material their children may be seeing and/or hearing.

Disasters and Trauma

There are two types of trauma that can occur in most disasters:

Individual Trauma can be defined as "a blow to the psyche that breaks through one's defenses so suddenly and with such brutal force that one cannot react to it effectively". Individual trauma manifests itself in the stress and grief reactions that are experienced by individual survivors.

Collective Trauma can be defined as "a blow to the basic tissues of social life that damages the bonds attaching people together and impairs the prevailing sense of community." Collective trauma severs the social ties that survivors have with each other and with their local community. These could be ties that might provide important psychological support in times of stress. Disasters disrupt nearly all the activities of daily living as well as the connections they entail. People may relocate to temporary housing away from neighbors, and other social support systems such as church, clinics, childcare, or recreation programs. Work can be disrupted or lost due to business failure, lack of transportation, loss of tools, or a worker's inability to concentrate due to the stress resulting from the disaster. Children may lose friends and school relationships as a result of the relocation. Fatigue and irritability can increase family conflict and undermine family relationships and ties.

For mental health professionals who are trained to work with individuals, collective trauma may often be less "visible". People will find it difficult, if not impossible, to heal from the effects of individual trauma while the community around them remains in shreds and there is no existing community setting.

People generally pull together and function during and after a disaster. However, their effectiveness is diminished. There are many types of stressors that affect disaster survivors. In the early "heroic" and "honeymoon" stages, there is a lot of energy, optimism, and altruism. However, while there is often a high level of activity, there is also a low level of efficiency. As the implications and the meaning of losses become more real, grief reactions intensify. Fatigue sets in. Frustrations and disillusionment accumulate and more stress symptoms may appear. Diminished cognitive functioning (short-term memory, confusion, difficulty setting priorities and making decisions, etc.) may occur due to fatigue and stress. This can impair survivors' abilities to make sound decisions and take necessary steps toward recovery and reconstruction.

Disaster stress and grief reactions are normal responses to an abnormal situation. Most disaster survivors are normal persons. They function reasonably well with the stresses and responsibilities of everyday life. However, with the added stress of disaster, many people will exhibit signs of emotional and psychological strain. Reactions include post-traumatic stress and grief responses. These are normal reactions to an extraordinary and abnormal situation. They are to be expected considering the circumstances. These reactions can be experienced by survivors, community residents, and disaster workers alike. They are usually transient in nature and rarely imply a serious mental disturbance or mental illness. Contrary to myth, neither post-traumatic stress disorder nor pathological grief reactions are rampant following disasters.

The post-traumatic stress process is a dynamic one. It is a process in which the survivor attempts to integrate a traumatic event into his/her self-structure. This process is natural and adaptive. It should not be labeled pathological (i.e., a "disorder") unless it is prolonged, blocked, exceeds a tolerable quality, or interferes with regular functioning to a significant extent.

Grief reactions are also a normal part of disaster recovery. Individuals may lose loved ones, homes, and treasured possessions. They may also lose hopes, dreams, and their assumptions about life and its meaning. Grief responses to such losses are common. They are not pathological (warranting therapy or counseling) unless the grief is an intensification, a prolongation, or an inhibition of normal grief.

Equilibrium usually re-establishes itself with the relief from stress, the ability to talk about the experience and the passage of time. Public information about normal reactions, education about ways to handle them, and early attention to symptoms that are problematic can speed recovery and prevent long-term problems.

"The Second Disaster"

The process of obtaining temporary housing, replacing belongings, getting permits to rebuild, applying for government assistance, seeking insurance reimbursement, and acquiring help from private or voluntary agencies is often fraught with rules, red tape, hassles, delays, and disappointment. People must often establish ties to bureaucracies to get aid they can get nowhere else. However, the organizational style of the aid-giving bureaucracies is often too impersonal for victims in the emotion-charged aftermath of the disaster. To complicate things still further, disasters and their special circumstances often foul up the bureaucratic procedures even of organizations established to handle disasters. Families are forced to deal with organizations that seem or are impersonal, inefficient, and inept.

Many individuals may be unable to obtain benefits for which they are eligible in a timely manner from the agencies involved. Individuals who felt competent and effective before the disaster may suddenly experience a serious erosion of self-esteem and confidence. Feelings of helplessness and anger are common. In response, mental health professionals may assist individuals by reassuring them that this "second disaster" is a common phenomenon. They can reassure them that most people have difficulty finding their way through the bureaucracy. Simply hearing the phrase "the second disaster" often brings a wave of relief to survivors, possibly with some welcomed laughter.

Mental Health Services

Unfortunately, many people equate the phrase "mental health services" with being "crazy". Offering mental health assistance to a disaster survivor might seem to be adding insult to injury—"First I have lost everything and now you think I'm mentally unstable." Most disaster survivors are overwhelmed by the time-consuming activities of putting the concrete aspects of their lives back together. Counseling or support groups may seem esoteric in the face of such pragmatic pressures. Some very effective mental health assistance can be provided while the worker is helping survivors with concrete tasks. For example, a mental health worker can use skilled but unobtrusive interviewing techniques to help a survivor in sorting out demands and setting priorities while they are sifting through rubble together.

People may be too busy cleaning up their homes or with other concrete demands to seek out services and programs that might help them. Initially, they are relieved to be alive and well. They often underestimate the financial impact and implication of their losses. They also tend to overestimate their available resources. The bottom-line impact of losses is often not evident for many months, or, occasionally, for years.

The heroism, altruism and optimism exhibited in the early stages of disaster might make it seem like "others are so much worse off than I am." For most people, there is a strong need to feel self-reliant and in control. Some people equate government relief programs as welfare. For others, especially recent immigrants who may have fled their countries of origin due to war or oppression, government is not to be trusted. Pride may be an issue for some people. They may feel ashamed that help is needed, or may not want help from "outsiders". Tact and sensitivity to these issues are important.

Most survivors of disaster are people who are temporarily disrupted by a severe stress. However, they can function capably under normal circumstances. A lot of the mental health work initially will be to give concrete types of help. Mental health professionals can assist survivors with problem-solving and decision making. They can help them to identify specific concerns, set priorities, explore alternatives, seek out resources, and choose a plan of action. Mental health staff must inform themselves about resources available to survivors, including local organizations and agencies in addition to specialized disaster relief resources. Mental health professionals may help directly with some problems, such as providing information, filling out forms, helping with cleanup, locating health care or child care, finding transportation. They may also make referrals to specific resources, such as assistance with loans, housing, employment, permits, etc.

Less frequently, individuals may experience more serious psychological responses such as severe depression, disorientation, immobilization, or an exacerbation of prior mental disturbance. These situations will likely require referral for more intensive psychological counseling. *The role of the disaster mental health professional is not to provide treatment for severely disturbed individuals directly. Their role is to recognize their needs and help link them with an appropriate treatment resource.*

Communities

The demographics and characteristics of the affected communities must be considered when designing a disaster mental health program. Urban, suburban and rural areas have different needs, resources, traditions and values about giving and receiving help. It is essential that programs consider the ethnic and cultural groups in the community, and provide services that are culturally relevant and in the languages of the people. Disaster recovery services are best accepted and utilized if they are integrated into existing, trusted community agencies and resources. In addition, programs are most effective if workers indigenous to the community and to its various ethnic and cultural groups are integrally involved in service delivery.

The traditional, office-based approach is of little use in disasters. Very few people will come to an office or approach a desk or table labeled "mental health". Generally, the goal is to provide *human services* for problems accompanied by emotional strain. It is essential not to use words which might imply emotional problems, such as counseling, therapy, psychiatric, psychological, neurotic, or psychotic. Mental health staff may identify themselves as human service workers, crisis counselors, or use other terminology that does not imply that their focus is on pathology. Workers seem less threatening when they refer to their services as "assistance", "support", or "talking" rather than labeling themselves as "mental health counselors".

Mental health professionals need to use an active outreach approach. They must go out to community sites where survivors are involved in the activities of their daily lives. Such places include neighborhoods, schools, disaster shelters, Disaster Application Centers (DACs), meal sites, hospitals, churches, community centers, etc. Survivors will usually be eager to talk about what happened to them when approached with warmth and genuine interest. Mental health outreach workers should not hold back from talking with survivors out of fear of "intruding" or invading their privacy. This approach can be referred to among workers as MHBWA (Mental Health By Walking Around).

Interventions

It is important for disaster mental health professionals to recognize the different stages of disaster and the varying psychological and emotional reactions involved in each stage. For example, it would be counterproductive to probe for feelings when shock and denial are shielding the survivor from intense emotions. Once the individual has mobilized internal and external coping resources, they are better able to deal with their feelings about the situation. During the "heroic" and "honeymoon" stages, people who have not lost loved ones may be feeling euphoric, altruistic and optimistic rather than bereaved. During the "inventory" phase, people are seeking and discussing the facts about the disaster, trying to piece reality together and understand what has happened. They may be more invested in discussing their thoughts than talking about feelings. In the "disillusionment" stage, people will likely be expressing feelings of frustration and anger. It is not usually a good time to ask if they can find something "good" that has happened to them through their experience.

Most people are willing and even eager to talk about their experiences in a disaster. However, it is important to respect the times when an individual may <u>not</u> want to talk about how things are going. Talking with a person in crisis does not mean always talking about the crisis. People usually "titrate their dosage" when dealing with pain and sorrow, and periods of normalcy and respite are also important. Talking about ordinary events and laughing at humorous points is also healing. If in doubt, <u>ask</u> the person whether they are in the mood to talk.

Support Systems

Disaster relocation and the intense activity involved in disaster recovery can disrupt people's interactions with their support systems. Encouraging people to make time for family and friends is important. Emphasizing the importance of "rebuilding relationships" in addition to rebuilding structures can be a helpful analogy.

The most important group for individuals is the family. Workers should attempt to keep the family together (in shelters and temporary housing, for example). Family members should be involved as much as possible in each other's recovery.

For people with limited support systems, disaster groups can be helpful. Support groups can help to counter isolation. People who have been through the same kind of situation feel they can truly understand one another. Groups can help to counter the myths of uniqueness and pathology. People find assurances that they are not alone or "weird" in their reactions reassuring. Groups not only provide emotional support, but survivors can share concrete information and recovery tips. They can benefit from the guidance of other experienced survivors. Besides the catharsis of sharing their experiences, they can identify with others who <u>are</u> recovering. They can then begin to feel hope for their own situation. Mental health professionals might involve themselves in setting up self-help support groups for survivors. They may also help facilitate support groups.

Finally, mental health professionals may also involve themselves in community organization activities. Community organization brings together community members to deal with concrete issues of concern to them. These issues might include social policy in disaster reconstruction or disaster preparedness at the neighborhood level. This process can assist survivors with disaster recovery by not only helping with concrete problems, but by re-establishing feelings of control, competence, self-confidence, and effectiveness. Possibly most important, it can help to re-establish social bonds and support networks that have been fractured by the disaster.

Role of The Mental Health Professional in Disasters

In the course of their work, most mental health professionals serve as consultants and supervisors to other professionals, trainees, residents and paraprofessionals. Disaster work almost always requires training, supervision, and consultation of human service workers, many of whom have little or no training. The professionals are likely to find that one of their major responsibilities is consultation.

Consultants are usually skilled in the clinical application of help to people with mental and emotional disorders. Consultees are individuals or groups of individuals working in an agency or organization in the community dealing with the specialized needs of people. Examples of such individuals are volunteers, paraprofessionals, school teachers, ministers, disaster agency workers, social welfare workers, housing specialists, law enforcement staff, and others. The primary role of the workers is not to provide mental health services as such, but to assist people whose reaction to stress is emotional distress. Consultation is usually organized around a current work problem identified by the consultees, or it may be related to future planning within an agency.

Most of the time, consultation is done with a group rather than with individual consultees. Consultants need to use their group skills to encourage group involvement. When case situations are presented, the consultants should make sure that one person does not remain the focus of the consultation and that others actively participate so that the group becomes an educational process for all members.

Purposes

In the initial steps of consultation, consultants have two main purposes:

- To explore the mental health needs of the people as the consultees see them, and
- To enhance the present system for more effective service to the community.

The consultants should keep in mind that they are outsiders in the consultee's system. They must be willing to absorb negative as well as positive emotional reactions to their presence. Any initial problems can be overcome if:

- the consultants demonstrate their interest and involvement in the worker's situation;
- the consultants invite and encourage the other's participation and show consideration for the other's feelings; and
- the consultants maintain and demonstrate their respect for the skills and "professionalism" of the consultees.

Objectives

The consultants' basic objective is to provide the disaster workers with knowledge they can integrate into their own tasks. To accomplish this, consultants:

1. **Provide Information:** The consultants need to provide the workers with information about mental health counseling and getting the person to participate in the process. Workers need to be informed about trouble signs and know about available help to

which they can send an individual or a family. Consultants should be as specific and clear as possible in any advice they offer and avoid confusing workers with too many or too involved explanations.

2. **Assist Workers:** Consultants need to help workers fulfill their own responsibilities. For example, if the workers' responsibilities are to extend outreach services for case finding, the consultants try to help them and, at the same time, to be sensitive to the mental health of their clients.
3. **Demonstrate Interventions:** Consultants may see individuals or groups within the workers' own systems and use the opportunity to demonstrate helpful techniques. For example, workers may want the consultants to see a disaster relief applicant who is tearful and non-communicative. Consultants may do so and share techniques and supportive behavior with the consultees. Another example is an evacuation shelter where the Red Cross is assisting distressed families and children. Consultants can lead a demonstration group in a joint activity, with the Red Cross workers as co-leaders.

Burnout

One of the primary responsibilities of consultants is to alert workers to the possibility of burnout, both in themselves and in their colleagues. Burnout is a condition frequently experienced by workers involved in disaster relief and related activities and often occurs among those working with children and families. Burnout is the normal result of increased demands and overwork after a disaster occurs. It appears as physical and emotional exhaustion, unrelieved feelings of fatigue, and marked irritability, and it decreases the individual's desire to work effectively.

Overwork and over-commitment are primarily responsible for the occurrence of burnout. After a disaster, workers make extreme demands on themselves as they try to help the victims. Even after this emergency phase has passed and they return to their regular jobs, many workers continue their disaster relief work, exhausting themselves in the process. Burnout may thus appear early or well into the post-disaster period.

1. Symptoms

Symptoms appear in at least four areas. Some people may develop just a few. Others may develop many.

- **Thinking:** Thinking ability slows, confusion appears, and workers cannot seem to make their usual good judgments and decisions, cannot set priorities, nor evaluate their own functioning objectively.
- **Body Symptoms:** Symptoms include physical exhaustion and fatigue; sleep difficulties (inability to fall asleep and/or to sleep through the night); stomach and digestion problems, such as loss of appetite or compulsive eating; loss of energy; tremors; many minor physical complaints.
- **Behavioral Signs:** Signs are: restlessness, agitation, nervousness, inability to sit still, apathy, withdrawal, loss of ability to move, loss of ability for self-expression, either by talking or writing, slips of the tongue, staggering gait.
- **Feelings and Mood:** Feelings include depression, irritability, anxiety, easily triggered and excessive rage, guilt, ready overexcitement.

2. Management

The first step is to be aware of, to be alert for, and to recognize the symptoms when they begin to appear. The earlier they are recognized the better. All personnel need to be instructed about the early symptoms so that they may recognize burnout not only in themselves, but also in their fellow workers. Any such observations should be reported to supervisors who should then talk to the individuals and try to get them to recognize the symptoms in themselves.

The supervisors should first attempt to persuade the helpers to take time off, but, if necessary, they should order it. Guilt over leaving the activity can be relieved by receiving official permission to stop and by being shown how they are no longer helping because of the loss of their effectiveness. They can be reassured that they will be welcomed on their return, their duties will be covered while they are absent, and that they will have improved greatly as a result of their short interruption in service.

Working With Disaster and Trauma Cross-Culturally

When disaster workers seek to assist with disasters in another country or culture it is essential that they have an understanding of the cultural norms and expectations of the population they hope to assist (Marsella, Friedman & Gerrity, 1996). How different cultural and ethnic groups handle and deal with stress, their abilities, needs and desires for certain types of assistance, motivations, sense of honor and pride, religious orientations and beliefs, political systems and leadership, and ways of handling and dealing with grief and loss are just some of the variables affected by cultural and ethnic differences (Mak & Nadelson, 1996).

Counseling and working with victims and workers in another culture present disaster and trauma workers some significant challenges. A necessary component shared by therapists of different orientations and cultures is the ability to generate perceptions of competence and concern in their clients (Torrey, 1972). Wrenn (1962) was one of the first to sensitize counselors to the problem of cultural encapsulation. He cautioned against the imposition of culturally alien goals, values and practices on clients across cultural lines. In the conduct of psychotherapy, it is important to take into account the respective cultural context and relate it to the needs, expectations, models and opportunities experienced in that culture (Draguns, 1975; Neki, 1973; Wittkower & Warner, 1974). Some non-western cultures rely to a greater extent than western ones on the induction of altered states of consciousness to help bring about catalytic effects needed to facilitate therapy. Two examples of procedures which are indigenous to their culture, yet developed and practiced by modern mental health professionals are Morita Therapy (Miura & Usa, 1970; Reynolds, 1976) and Naikan Therapy (Tanaka-Matsumi, 1979) in Japan. Regardless of the technique used, the role of the therapist is catalytic, enabling the client to make use of his/her existing assets and strengths (Prince, 1976, 1980). It is important to point out that therapy and counseling services which are geared to a culturally distinct group have to be appropriate in process and in goals to be acceptable and effective (Sue, 1977).

The most common symptoms displayed across cultures in various disasters are those associated with the diagnoses of depression, anxiety and PTSD (Lechat, 1990; de la Fuente, 1990; Zhang & Zhang, 1991; Lima et al, 1990; Joh, 1997; Canino, Bravo, Rubio-Stipec, & Woodbury, 1990; Guarnaccia, 1993). They manifest themselves in different ways within cultures and ethnic groups, but the symptoms fit the general diagnostic criteria for depression, anxiety disorders, and PTSD. Dealing with these in culturally relevant counseling contexts is the task faced by cross-cultural counselors providing disaster mental health services and psychological first aid.

Assessment

Maslow (1987) has presented a hierarchy of needs which can be a useful guide and model for assessing the general needs and developmental stages of individuals and countries, cultural and ethnic groups. His model for universal human development provides a focus and culture-specific approach to providing mental health services in cross-cultural settings. Taylor (1998) presents an example of some of the factors involved in understanding cultural differences prior to offering psychosocial services. He outlines his approach to providing services following a very destructive cyclone in the Cook Islands in 1997. He also discusses a number of other situations in which cultural diversity is a major factor. Variables and other considerations involved in providing cross-cultural counseling in disaster settings are reviewed by Doherty (1999).

A useful assessment model for evaluating immediate individual levels of functioning following a disaster or other traumatic event is one proposed by Lazarus (1976, 1989, 2000). He used the acronym BASIC-ID (Behavior, Affect, Somatic concerns, Imagery, Cognition, Interpersonal Skills, Drugs) to outline a multi-modal behavioral approach which can be adapted for use in disaster trauma situations and can be adapted cross-culturally. It is important to identify the normal responses within the cultural context for each of the BASIC-ID components so as not to impose the perceptions of the assessor on the client. For example, emotional and behavioral responses in one cultural context might be considered inappropriate within another. General symptoms can be listed for each component. Development of similar lists for different cultural groups could be helpful for those mental health professionals who might be responding to traumatic events and disasters in another culture. Providing such information to responders as part of their briefings prior to deployment would help them to provide culturally relevant responses.

Some Conclusions

Managing disaster situations is difficult at best. Strategies for improving international and other cross-cultural disaster operations can help develop and provide more effective responses. It is important to learn from crisis events, coordinate international/cross-cultural disaster assistance, provide adequate and accurate information in disaster environments, learn how to take appropriate actions, and develop trust in disaster operations (Comfort, 1989; Paton, 1996).

The real trauma of cultural diversity is partially the stress experienced by well-meaning responders who are continually searching for ways to respond effectively cross-culturally. Counselors should have knowledge of the culture they work in as part of their expertise and competence. Giordano and Giordano (1976) provided some very valuable and specific information to keep in mind when initiating and maintaining contact with clients of another culture. The knowledge of the culture of one's clients provides the counselor with an entree and/or point of departure. The experience of the counselor with a cultural group or the information on it in the relevant professional literature serves as a source of hypotheses, to be verified, discarded and/or modified based on acquisition of further information. Working together with a counselor/healer from the culture could vastly improve the probability of success in appropriate interventions. This would be of special concern in a disaster, critical incident response, or other trauma situation.

In order to achieve the goals of providing appropriate and adequate cross-cultural disaster mental health services, it's essential for providers to establish collaborative supportive international and cross-cultural relationships (Ring & Vazquez, 1993). Development of a general model of international and cross-cultural disaster mental health services with a strong emphasis on cross-cultural variables and with plans for response based on the needs, beliefs and desires of different countries and cultures is encouraged. Consultation and collaboration with providers and planners in other countries and cultures together with development of in-country disaster response plans along with a strong educational component can help mitigate disaster mental health related responses and problems.

Mental Health Roles In The Emergency Operations Center

Part 1 – EOC Functions and Incident Command

In times of serious emergencies and disasters, organizational coordination and communication are required beyond that needed in more routine situations. The Emergency Operations Center (EOC) facilitates this communication. The EOC is usually under the jurisdiction of the local government. The jurisdiction's emergency management office is responsible for its maintenance and operation. If the disaster needs escalate beyond the capacity of local resources, the governor may be requested to declare a state level of emergency. At this point, state resources are made available to the local jurisdiction. In such a situation, a state EOC may be activated. An EOC is activated, operated, and closed according to a preplanned set of policies and procedures (Herman, 1982).

The EOC is usually a pre-designated site or facility. It is equipped and supplied prior to the need for its operation. It is located away from the disaster scene, usually in or near governmental offices in order to have access to needed records and resources. Many older EOCs are located underground with construction designed to protect the facility from radioactive as well as natural and technological hazards. However, there is no longer a perceived need for this. Most newer EOCs are built above ground. EOCs are usually designed to be self-sufficient for a reasonable period of time with provisions for electricity, water, sewage disposal, ventilation, and security. Food storage, preparation, and serving facilities are desirable, as well as a bunk room or cots for tired personnel. The EOC may have different rooms and areas for different functions.

Ideally, each organization or agency has a clearly designated worksite with communication equipment and status boards for recording information pertinent to the organization's area of responsibility. For example, social service/shelter operations will maintain a status board listing sites of open shelters and numbers of occupants and staff.

The EOC is different from a *command post* in two respects. First, the EOC is not usually at the site of the event or incident. A command post is a facility at the scene of an emergency or disaster where site operations are directed. There may be multiple sites of impact and multiple command posts. Each command post has direct communications with the EOC. Second, the EOC facilitates overall, system-wide coordination of response among many disaster organizations. It does not focus on detailed operations at specific sites.

EOC Functions

Functions of the EOC include information management, situation assessment, and resource allocation. These functions include:

- Providing a common location of operation for individuals having top management responsibilities during the response and early recovery phase; providing centralized direction and control.
- Ensuring clear delegation of responsibility and authority and establishing a clear chain of command.
- Serving as the single point for collection, evaluation, display, and dissemination of information; ensuring that decision makers in the EOC and in the field have adequate and accurate information.
- Coordinating personnel, supplies, and equipment on a priority basis.
- Providing communication and direction to external response agencies.
- Assessing the need for additional assistance such as mutual aid or requests to the governor for state and/or federal assistance.
- Ensuring that affected populations are evacuated and sheltered.
- Monitoring the situation and relaying warnings to local officials and the public.
- Providing accurate public information and rumor control.

Incident Command System in the EOC

In order to be able to carry out their diverse responsibilities and activities, EOCs must have a system in place. The strategy most commonly used is the Incident Command System (ICS). ICS is an on-scene emergency response system developed by the fire service and is being increasingly integrated into other emergency organizations and private industry. It provides for basic direction and control, including decision making and coordination among multiple agencies (Drabek and Hoetmer, 1991). it provides a chain of command which adapts to emergency events both large and small. Additionally, it provides a common management terminology during times of stress (Russell, 1991).

It is an organizational structure which is divided into four sections: operations, planning, logistics, and finance.

- **Planning** involves acquiring information about current and future situations.
- **Operations** directs activities to reduce the immediate hazard and to maintain and/or restore essential functions.
- **Logistics** provides for all support needs such as food, communications, medical supplies, etc.
- **Finance** tracks all costs.

The functions can be performed by separate individuals simultaneously, or one individual can perform two or more functions (Russell, 1991).

EOC Staffing

The characteristics of the community, the size and scope of the emergency, and the phase of the response determines which individuals need to be in the EOC at any point in time.

Individuals who are needed in the EOC in the early stages of the emergency might not be the same people needed during later stages. In the early stages, the EOC will likely be operating 24 hours a day. This requires coverage for multiple shifts.

Though the local government has overall responsibility for disaster response, a variety of other public, private, and voluntary agencies may be represented. Groups which are commonly represented include:

- Elected officials and top appointed officials
- Office of Emergency Services personnel
- Public safety (local and state police, county sheriff, fire, emergency medical services, 911 communications)
- Public works
- Public health
- Mental health
- Social service/shelter operations (including public social services, American Red Cross, Salvation Army, etc.)
- Coroner
- Schools
- Public utilities
- Public information officer
- Amateur radio volunteers
- Resource procurement personnel
- Finance personnel
- Support staff (food, janitorial, clerical, stress-management)

EOC representatives may be of two types: those with emergency decision-making responsibilities and those who serve a liaison function with other agencies and jurisdictions. It is vital that EOC representatives responsible for decision-making come from the top levels of management, representing the top person or second-in-command in their organization (Herman, 1982), or have been authorized to make decisions on top management's behalf. Coordination can be hampered when representatives at an EOC lack the full authority to make command and coordination decisions. Unfortunately, those assigned to the EOC often represent middle management levels of their organizations. Mid-level managers often do not have the authority or experience required for emergency decision-making. It is essential that the EOC representative have in-depth knowledge of the capabilities of his/her organization and how its resources can best be activated. Retrospective analyses of emergency operations have shown that each representative must have sufficient rank and authority to make immediate, high-level policy decisions (Auf der Heide, 1989). In a declared emergency, the local emergency ordinance can give mid-level managers the necessary authority.

The EOC is likely to have one or more support staff who provide services and supplies that keep the organization running. These staff may provide clerical support, switchboard functions, food and beverages, maintenance and janitorial services, and stress management.

Ideally, each agency represented at the EOC should use a team approach to manage shift coverage and any unexpected leave of absence. Orderly rotation of personnel is essential for decreasing the probability of dangerous errors due to fatigue. Additionally, a team approach acknowledges the value of rest and interdependency as characteristics of successful emergency management.

Shift change procedures should ensure communication and continuity between shifts. New shifts should be briefed on operations of the prior shift. An action log can provide the incoming shift with brief written documentation of decisions and activities of the prior shift.

Mental Health Role in the EOC

Not all jurisdictions' emergency plans call for a mental health representative in the EOC. Most municipal jurisdictions do not have a mental health department. In many county and state jurisdictions, mental health is a division of a larger department, such as Health Services or Human Services. In such cases, emergency plans often call for the department head to be present in the EOC. Mental health, as a subordinate division, is not represented.

It is, however, strongly recommended that emergency management plans include a decision-making representative of mental health in the EOC. Representation legitimizes the importance of mental health's role both in the EOC and in the community-wide recovery efforts. It ensures that mental health resources are used appropriately.

The mental health EOC representative should be an individual who is specifically knowledgeable in the field of disaster mental health. This individual must also have the authority to make key decisions. He/she must have access to the most accurate information available in order to deploy mental health resources most efficiently and effectively. This individual must also be aware of decisions and actions of other agencies with whom mental health must coordinate efforts. He/she must also have information about decisions of other organizations that may affect mental health operations. Examples include such things as road closures that will affect mental health's access to an area, or the opening of additional shelters that will require mental health staffing. In addition, mental health expertise may be important to other key decision makers when there are mental consequences of particular decisions or actions. For example, a decision to provide mass shelter in separate facilities for men and women will violate the basic disaster mental health principle that families are a key source of stability for individuals, and family units should remain intact.

In the EOC, the mental health work station should be situated close to representatives from public health, emergency medical services, social services, the Red Cross, and schools. In some EOCs, these functions work together at the same table or in a room designated specifically for them. Mental health will also need to work with the coroner if there have been deaths, in order to ensure outreach and emotional support to the bereaved and, in some cases, to the coroner's staff. The disaster mental health plan may call for mental health to provide support to first responders in the field (fire, EMS, law enforcement). If so, the mental health EOC representative should work in close coordination with first responder representatives in the EOC to ensure that services are delivered where needed.

The responsibility of the mental health representative is to make decisions about priorities and resource allocation, in coordination with other agencies represented. He/she also serves as advisor to the top official in charge of the EOC (usually the County Administrative Officer or the Office of Emergency Services Director).

The mental health representative in the EOC provides overall direction of the disaster mental health response. His/her responsibilities are executive in nature. They are designed to develop. direct, and maintain a viable organization and to keep that organization coordinated with other agencies, elected officials, and the public. As outlined by Auf der Heide (1989), these responsibilities include:

- Organizing to meet the needs of the disaster.
- Establishing disaster mental health response objectives.
- Setting priorities for work accomplishments.
- Approving resource and personnel orders and releases.
- Approving public information outputs.
- Coordinating with agencies and public officials.

In all but the smallest jurisdictions, the mental health system will need a disaster services *field coordinator* who will function outside the EOC. This will most likely be at the mental health administrative office or alternate location. It is the responsibility of this coordinator to manage the deployment of staff and provision of services in the field according to the directives of the EOC representative. This coordinator is responsible for keeping the EOC representative informed of mental health activities and needs for personnel, supplies, and equipment. The field coordinator also feeds information about conditions in the field back to the EOC.

In very large mental health organizations, the EOC representative and field coordinator may require additional coordinators for planning and logistical functions. A *planning coordinator* collects data and provides the coordinator and EOC representative with information about the incident. Information includes status of resources, status of situations, and estimates of future needs for the coming days and weeks. The planning coordinator may also conduct planning meetings, prepare alternative strategies, and compile action plans. The planning coordinator collects data for and may prepare grant applications to FEMA for a Disaster Crisis Counseling Grant as authorized by PL 100-707, Section 416.

A *logistics coordinator* handles the pragmatic aspects of deploying personnel, equipment, and services in the field. This includes providing the services that "keep the organization going", such as communications, food, shelter, security, and debriefing for mental health staff in the field. Additionally, the logistics coordinator ensures adequate facilities, supplies, service equipment, and other resources needed by staff in the field to conduct their business (Auf der Heide, 1989). In very large-scale disasters, military support may be necessary to provide logistical support.

Communication between the EOC and mental health staff in the field may be hampered if phones are inoperable. Cell phones may be valuable in areas with such service. Mental health might also consider establishing a cooperative agreement with amateur radio ("HAM") groups. Many of them routinely provide radio communication for such groups as the Red Cross. With such an agreement, radio operators at the EOC and key mental health locations could provide the needed communication linkage. Hand-held radios can be a valuable asset in the field.

Mental Health Support in the EOC

Drabek and Hoetmer (1991) state that "No kitchen generates the kind of heat found in the EOC." The social and psychological context within which life and death decisions are made generates pressure that is immense.

There is an ever-present need to take immediate action to prevent or alleviate human suffering and physical destruction. This pressure is intensified by scrutiny of the media and public officials. The pressures are increased further by the shortage of time. During the disaster, decisions must usually be made quickly if they are to have any effect at all.

The climate of the EOC is also influenced by limited, uncertain, rapidly changing, and often conflicting information. Available information tends to be partial and imperfect.

Priorities for action may shift rapidly as new information is presented. The principle priorities for emergency management are to minimize loss of life, personal injury, and property damage. The actions that support these priorities, however, may change during the course of the event. For example, a levee may fail during a river flood, endangering a different part of town. A previously safe shelter may become damaged in earthquake aftershocks, requiring the opening of a new shelter and the movement of evacuees.

Additionally, the EOC climate embodies the stress that arises from overlapping lines of authority and responsibility. Inter-organizational relationships in disaster necessitate resource sharing and collaborative dependence. If authority or responsibility is unclear, performance may be slow when time pressures are great and response demands are high. The potential for conflict and frustration is high both in the EOC and in the field.

Drabek and Hoetmer (1991) further describe some of the unique stresses that affect emergency personnel in the EOC. Staff literally cannot move around much. They are often confined to a table or work station and its communication devices. They receive information about the entire scope of the disaster, no matter where it occurs. Therefore, they are acutely aware of the extent of loss and suffering. They have no direct contact with disaster victims and cannot look an individual in the face and feel personally responsible for providing help.

Essentially, the EOC climate is high-pressured and emotionally charged. The level of stress must be managed if reasonable and effective decisions are to be made quickly. Training, planning, and regular exercises or drills can prepare staff to function in such an environment. Additionally, a pre-planned stress management component provided by experienced disaster mental health workers in the EOC can help personnel to manage stress so that it does not interfere with functioning.

Stress Management

In addition to the executive role of mental health in the EOC, mental health representatives may provide a support function to EOC staff through the provision of stress management interventions. Such support may be in observing, advising, and intervening with disaster-related stress among the EOC personnel.

If the EOC isn't too hectic, the decision-making representative may wear two hats and may provide this support. However, in disasters of large size or long duration, the decision-making representative will be too busy managing the mental health response to the disaster to provide stress management services in the EOC. It is recommended, therefore, that a mental health staff member(s) skilled in stress management be assigned as support staff to the

EOC. It is preferable that these individuals have had training and experience in disaster mental health.

The role of mental health support staff must be understood by other staff in the EOC. It is ideal that the staff member be introduced and his/her role explained by the top official in charge of the EOC. It would be helpful for the mental health representative to write the script for the EOC director. This will help ensure that the role is accurately and appropriately defined. It communicates that the role is seen as important and that it has the sanction of the person in charge.

Managers who have EOC responsibilities in disasters should have pre-disaster training regarding disaster worker stress management. They should be aware of the common stressors affecting managers of disasters and to the stress reactions they are likely to experience. Stress management and coping strategies which are effective in such settings can be taught. Policies and procedures need to be established pre-disaster to help mitigate stressors and to help personnel manage their own stress and fatigue. For example, the recommended policy for rest periods is one break every two to four hours. It is recommended that shifts be no longer than 12 hours in duration followed by 12 hours of time off. If possible, a full 24-hour day off should be scheduled after each seven-to-ten day shift of work. These policies should be explained as proven standards that enable personnel to function at a higher level of effectiveness for a longer period, Covering these policies and procedures in pre-disaster training can instill them as a normal part of the EOC routine. It can also prevent personnel from feeling unfairly singled out when a break is suggested during EOC operations (Mitchell and Bray, 1990).

Mental Health Roles In The Emergency Operations Center

Part 2 – Individuals and Environment

Mental health staff should be concerned with two levels in addressing the needs of EOC staff: ***(1) the individuals and (2) the environment.***

Individual Interventions

The mental health role when working with individuals in the EOC is that of an observer and advisor. The mental health representative can be particularly helpful when the effectiveness of other staff members has become diminished due to fatigue and stress. Common signs to look for include cognitive difficulties such as confusion, memory problems, difficulty making calculations or setting priorities, and difficulty making decisions. People may become moody, irritable, or lose their temper. Some individuals may experience physical symptoms such as headaches, back pain, and tense muscles. All of these are common human reactions in the abnormal situation of a disaster. Mental health workers need to assess these reactions in the context of the situation.

Myers and Zunin (1992) suggest that perhaps the most effective style of mental health intervention in an environment like the EOC is that of informally "roaming" through the worksite *(MHBWA – Mental Health By Walking Around)*. This involves circulating through the work units and break areas, chatting with people, providing brief interventions, giving ad hoc stress management education, assessing the environment for stressors, and occasionally making an "appointment" to see a person individually during a break. This has been called the "over-cup-of-coffee" style of intervention, in which stress management staff simply interact in a "therapeutic" manner with personnel. It has also been referred to as MHBWA (Mental Health By Walking Around). It has been demonstrated repeatedly that emergency-oriented staff respond best to an informal structure when engaging in interactions with stress management or mental health staff.

If a worker's stress is interfering with his/her functioning or is impeding the work of the group, a short break may be helpful in returning the individual to a higher level of functioning. Fifteen to 30 minutes in a room away from the stimuli of the work environment, with some food, beverages and perhaps some brief stress reduction activities, is often all that is needed. The mental health worker should suggest a break to the worker, and accompany the worker on his/her break if the worker does not object. This should be coordinated with the EOC manager so that coverage of the individual's functions can occur. Coverage for short breaks can be carried out by individuals with similar EOC functions (for example, one law enforcement representative covering for another). In cases where urgent decisions must be made, the break can always be interrupted.

Individual mental health interventions in such settings should be brief in nature. They are intended to return the individual to their role in the EOC. Ideally, a separate room should be available for an individual intervention. If this is not available, a brief walk outdoors or in a corridor may be used. Interventions should focus on the immediate situation and may include the following (adapted from Santa Barbara CISD Policies and Procedures, 1991):

- ASK what is happening with the individual now. What is the worst part of the situation for them? What will help right now?
- LISTEN AND REASSURE the individual that the feelings are normal under the circumstances. Offer supportive comments. Try to provide for the worker's stated needs.
- INFORM the worker that the purpose of the break is to get them back to work as soon as possible,
- SUGGEST STRESS MANAGEMENT strategies that might seem appropriate, such as deep breathing, progressive relaxation, gentle muscle stretching exercises, or "self-talk". Diversionary activities such as playing cards or reading a magazine for a short while may help. Food and beverage should be suggested if the worker has not eaten for awhile.
- LET THE WORKER REST. After chatting with the worker, the mental health worker should allow him/her some "breathing space" for 15 to 20 minutes. When checking back on the worker, mental health and the worker probably can determine whether the worker is ready and able to return to his/her work station.

There may be occasions when an EOC worker may be so fatigued or so distressed by the situation that a decision should be made to release the individual to go home. If the person is highly upset, the mental health worker will want to be sure that the person has safe transport home, and that someone be with them at home (Mitchell and Bray, 1990).

Mental health staff in the EOC serve in an advisory role to the EOC director. They may make recommendations to the director about individual staff members who may need to take a break or be relieved of duty until they are more rested. However, mental health staff have no authority to order any of these actions. That authority rests with the individual next in command above the affected staff member or with the EOC director.

When disaster personnel are in the "heroic phase" of response, they are often not aware of the effects of stress on their functioning. Specific feedback about their performance may need to be given to convince them that they need to rest. Often, workers may resist the suggestion that they take breaks or that they need time off-duty for rest. Workers may actually need to be ordered to take breaks. This is best accomplished by pointing out that the worker's role is vitally important, and that it is essential for him/her to rest in order to return to functioning at his/her full potential.

Mental health support staff need to circulate throughout the EOC and regularly check with other EOC representatives about the welfare of their field personnel. Department heads should be reminded about the importance of policies concerning breaks, length of shifts, etc. for field personnel. Mental health staff in the EOC need to make sure that linkages between field personnel and field mental health staff are in place to provide appropriate mental health support. Mental health support staff should not overlook 911 operators (whether functioning in or near the EOC, or in another facility).

Environmental Interventions

Mental health staff work with the EOC director and/or other support staff to ensure that, as much as possible, the EOC environment considers the psychosocial needs of the workers. Consultation might concern the physical environment, staff scheduling, or support and stress management services for EOC personnel.

The EOC is the "nerve center" of disaster operations. By definition, it is hectic and noisy. Situations change rapidly. Workers must adjust continuously to new information and new crises that require their attention. Mental health workers observe the environment and its activities, and advise the EOC director of any suggestions that might reduce the stress level. Consultation might concern EOC layout, with suggestions for noise reduction, traffic flow, groupings of workers, etc. A quiet room or space where workers can get away from the bustle of the EOC on their breaks should be suggested if one is not already designated. A separate room for individual mental health interventions may also be desirable. Adequate lighting, communication devices, supplies, etc. can all help reduce worker frustrations.

Basic needs of food, clothing, and shelter must be accommodated. Regular and healthy meals, snacks, and beverages need to be emphasized. Staff should be encouraged to avoid excessive caffeine and sugar. If staff are "living" in the EOC, arrangements for showers and clean clothing need to be made. Sleeping space should be made as comfortable and quiet as possible.

One major concern for EOC staff is the well-being of their family members. Most disaster plans encourage personnel to do what is necessary to ensure the well-being of their families prior to reporting for disaster duty. This may not always be possible for the high-ranking officials designated to staff the EOC. Sometimes, disaster conditions themselves may prevent personnel from learning the whereabouts and situation of their loved ones. If a mechanism is not in place to try to locate and learn the status of family members, mental health staff should consult with the EOC director about the importance of this function.

An EOC support staff member may be assigned the sole responsibility of locating families, using suggestions of EOC personnel as to individual family members' possible whereabouts, and using whatever communication systems are available.

It's recommended that jurisdictions establish policies urging family members to contact the work site by phone or by any other feasible means during the emergency. Additionally, the policy should require personnel to complete a chart or form with the likely whereabouts of their loved ones during various times of the day. Tranchina (1991) has noted that these policies can provide some reasonable means for organizations to assist in locating family members of staff during major emergencies or catastrophes. Knowledge of family status can help staff to perform their duties without the added burden of worrying about family members.

One major family concern for EOC representatives is the care of their children for the duration of their work responsibilities. Provision of childcare for EOC and other disaster personnel should be a high priority in order to allow personnel to function with as much peace of mind as possible. For example, the city of Oakland, California, as part of the city Emergency Plan, provides childcare on a 24-hour basis for children of emergency response personnel, including those working in the EOC. Trained childcare workers watch children at a location near the EOC, where personnel can visit their children during breaks and time-off (Renteria, 1992).

Mental health staff provide consultation to the EOC director about stress management interventions and activities for EOC personnel. Advice about scheduling of breaks and time-off can be important. Diversionary activities such as magazines, cards, or games can be provided for use during off-duty time. For example, in a busy EOC during the response to the Loma Prieta earthquake, a masseuse provided needed relief to knotted necks and shoulders.

The healing properties of humor should not be forgotten. Laughter can help break tension. It can provide relief from stress. It is not unusual for disaster jokes and cartoons to surface soon after a disaster. Disaster worksites often become decorated with cartoons that help workers keep some perspective and "lighten up" a bit in the midst of a difficult situation. Humor, however, must be used with some care. People are highly suggestible when under stress. Both workers and survivors can sometimes take things personally and may feel angry or hurt if they feel that they are personally the subject of a joke.

Pamphlets and/or video/audio tapes on stress reduction exercises should be provided. Mental health staff can help by teaching these techniques to personnel on or off-duty. Stress management "mini-breaks" can be conducted on-site during lulls in activity or during staff meetings or briefings. In 5-10 minute sessions, mental health staff can give brief talks on sources of stress, coping strategies, and stress management techniques (Myers and Zunin, 1992). They can then lead personnel through a few stress management activities, such as deep breathing or stretching tense muscles.

Mental health should also plan or provide stress management interventions for personnel after a shift in the EOC, after the EOC is deactivated, or after an individual's role in the EOC has ended. Ideally, the policies regarding these activities should be in place before the EOC is activated. Interventions and activities may include a shift-end defusing (mini-debriefing), a demobilization meeting for all personnel when the EOC is deactivated, a formal debriefing, a critique, and formal recognition of EOC staff's contribution to the disaster response.

A demobilization meeting can be provided for personnel when the EOC is shut down. Such a meeting is short in duration, about 30 minutes, and serves as a "transition" from the operation back into the world. Usually, information is given about stress and the typical signs and symptoms that people experience (Mitchell and Bray, 1990). Mental health staff emphasize stress management techniques such as eating well, getting rest and exercise, avoiding abuse of alcohol or drugs, and returning to a routine (Hartsough and Myers, 1985). Handouts on stress and its management should be given out. The person in charge, in this case the EOC director, should make closing comments, and thank personnel for their work (Ventura CISD policies and procedures, 1990; Mitchell and Bray, 1990). The meeting provides an opportunity for ventilation of feelings, but usually people are anxious to go home, and no one should be required to talk.

If the work has been highly stressful or traumatic for EOC personnel, a formal debriefing should be arranged for all EOC personnel who wish to attend. A debriefing is a meeting, led by a mental health facilitator with special training in the technique, which provides an organized approach to the management of stress responses in emergency services (Mitchell, 1983). The mental health staff member who has been working in the EOC will probably have become an "insider" to the EOC team. Debriefers should not have been participants in the situation they are debriefing. An outside facilitator should be used, and the EOC mental health personnel may attend the debriefing as "debriefees".

Different from a debriefing, but often equally important, is a critique of the operation. While a debriefing focuses on the psychological and emotional responses of workers, a critique is a meeting for analyzing and evaluating the effectiveness of the operation and recommending changes in policy and procedures for the future. Calling a critique is the responsibility of the EOC director. Mental health may suggest and encourage a critique, and may provide a facilitator. A critique can assure that the input of all participants is heard, and can be helpful in bringing closure to the operation. A critique and debriefing should not be combined in the same meeting, as agendas are quite different (Hartsough and Myers, 1985).

Following a disaster operation, formal recognition of the workers' participation can be very meaningful. Individuals in the EOC have usually worked long hours under grueling circumstances, and a letter in the individual's personnel file or a certificate of appreciation will be much appreciated. Following the Loma Prieta earthquake of 1989 and the Eastbay firestorm of 1991, several agencies chose to give lapel pins to their employees in recognition of their service. Staff wore them proudly, and they were appreciated much more than a certificate would have been (Renteria, 1992). EOC support staff and staff outside the EOC who "minded the store" while EOC staff were away from their regular jobs should also be included in the recognition. In situations where not all personnel are recognized, or where some agencies provide recognition and others do not, there can be feelings of disappointment and even dissent among personnel.

Summary

Because the field of disaster mental health is highly specialized, mental health jurisdictions should have disaster plans that are thoroughly integrated with the comprehensive emergency management plan of their jurisdiction. It is advisable that in a disaster of any magnitude a mental health representative with decision-making authority should be present in the EOC.

Mental health staff also play a vital role in providing stress-management functions for EOC personnel during and following EOC operations.

Selecting and Training Disaster Mental Health Staff

Skills and competencies that are required of disaster mental health workers are enough different from the typical inpatient/outpatient clinical practice to require more specialized selection and training. When a disaster strikes a community, having a cadre of specially trained mental health professionals who can be quickly mobilized, oriented, and deployed is critical. If the impacted area does not have this capacity, mutual aid agreements with those communities that have trained and experienced disaster mental health workers will be helpful in the chaotic times immediately following impact.

Predisaster Planning

Much of the confusion and stress present at the time of disaster impact can be eliminated when a mental health agency has a core staff pre-designated and trained as a disaster response team. Regular in-service training and participation in disaster exercises in the local jurisdiction can help maintain and fine tune skills. If the resources permit, the team can respond to smaller crises which occur in the jurisdiction. This will provide staff with some first-hand experience they can use when a larger disaster strikes.

Funds for training are hard to come by and sometimes non-existent. Training is considered a necessary and appropriate aspect of the Federal Emergency Management Agency (FEMA) Crisis Counseling programs, both in the Immediate and Regular Programs. Mental health planners and administrators should include realistic training budgets in their grant applications.

Selecting Disaster Mental Health Staff

Disaster mental health work is not for everyone. It is challenging and rewarding work which requires mental health professionals to be flexible and socially extroverted. Despite their altruism and sincere desire to help, *not all individuals are well-suited for disaster work.* Whether designating and training disaster staff prior to or during a disaster, the mental health manager should consider several selection issues.

Selection of professional or paraprofessional staff should consider the demographics of the disaster-affected population, including ethnicity and language; the personality characteristics and social skills of the staff member; the disaster phase; and the roles the worker may play in disaster response and recovery efforts. Workers who are selected for disaster response and recovery work should not be so severely impacted by the disaster that their responsibilities at home or their emotional reactions will interfere with participation in the program, or vice versa.

Population Demographics

Managers should choose staff who have special skills that match the needs of the population. For example, staff who have special expertise working with children and the local schools should be included. If there are many elderly persons in the community, the team should include persons skilled in working with older adults.

Ethnicity and Language

Survivors will react to and recover from disaster within the context of their ethnic background, cultural viewpoint, life experiences, and values. Those who have limited English-speaking skills may experience difficulty communicating needs and feelings except in their native language. All aspects of disaster operations must be sensitive to cultural issues, and services must be provided in ways that are culturally appropriate.

It is essential that mental health staff be both familiar and comfortable with the culture of the groups affected by the disaster. It is very desirable that they also be fluent in the languages of non-English speaking groups affected. Mental health staff should include individuals who are indigenous to specific cultural groups affected by the disaster. If such staff are not immediately available, mutual aid staff with the required ethnic backgrounds and language skills should be recruited from other community agencies or mental health jurisdictions for the immediate post-disaster phase. Indigenous personnel can be recruited and trained for the longer term recovery work at a later time.

Personality

The ability to remain focused and to respond appropriately are necessary qualities for individuals who participate directly in a disaster. Disaster mental health staff must be able to function well in confused, often chaotic environments. Workers must be able to "think on their feet", and have a common-sense, practical, flexible and often improvisational approach to problem-solving. They must be comfortable with changing situations. They must be able to function with role ambiguity, unclear lines of authority, and a minimum of structure. Many of the most successful disaster mental health workers perceive these factors as challenges rather than burdens. Initiative and stamina are required, as well as self-awareness and an ability to monitor and manage their own stress.

Workers need to be able to work cooperatively in a liaison capacity. They need to be aware of and comfortable with value systems and life experiences other than their own. An eagerness to reach out and explore the community to find people needing help, instead of a "wait and treat" attitude, is essential (Farberow and Frederick, 1978). Workers must enjoy people and not appear lacking in confidence. If the worker is shy or afraid, it will interfere with establishing a connection (DeWolfe, 1992). Staff must be comfortable initiating a conversation in any community setting. In addition, workers must be willing and able to "be with" survivors who may be suffering tragedy and enormous loss without being compelled to try to "fix" the situation.

Importance of Disaster Phases

In the immediate response phase of disaster, an "action orientation" is important. Workers who do well with the pace of crisis intervention do well in this phase. Personnel who have worked in emergency services in a local mental health center or a hospital emergency room are frequently well-suited to this phase of disaster work.

Some people cannot and do not function well when exposed to the sights and sounds of physical trauma. These staff should obviously not be asked to provide mental health services at the scene of injuries or in first aid stations, hospital emergency rooms, or morgues. This does not mean that they cannot be on the disaster response team. There are many other roles that they can play. Involved personnel should openly discuss such issues during initial formation of the team so that individuals best suited to these roles can be pre-designated.

Long-term mental health recovery programs, covering the period from about one month to one year post-disaster, are different in nature and pace from the immediate response phase. Mass care shelters and disaster application centers (DACs) are closed or closing. Locating disaster survivors is more difficult. Mental health workers need to be adept and creative with outreach in the community.

Results of outreach and education efforts are often difficult to measure. Survivors do not traditionally seek out mental health service. There are few "clients" to treat and count. Clinically oriented staff who are accustomed to an office-based practice often question their usefulness and effectiveness. "Action-oriented" staff who thrived in the immediate response phase may not enjoy or function well in the longer-term recovery phase where patience, perseverance, and an ability to function without seeing immediate results are assets.

Roles and Responsibilities of Disaster Mental Health Workers

Disaster mental health roles and responsibilities are diverse. Thoughtful matching of worker skills and personalities to the specific assignment can help ensure success of mental health efforts.

- *Outreach*: Working in neighborhoods, mass care shelters, disaster application centers, or other community settings requires workers who are adept at such non-traditional mental health approaches as "aggressive hanging out" and "over a cup of coffee" assessments and interventions.
- *Public education:* Public education efforts require staff who are interested and effective in public speaking and working with the media. Development of fliers and brochures requires good writing skills.
- *Community liaison:* Establishing and maintaining liaison with community leaders requires someone who understands and is effective in dealing with organizational dynamics and the political process. Working successfully in the "grass roots" community requires someone who understands the local culture, social network, formal and informal leadership, and is effective in establishing relationships at the neighborhood level. Liaison activities might include everything from attending grange or church gatherings, participating in neighborhood meetings, or providing disaster mental health consultation to government officials.
- *Crisis counseling:* For most disaster survivors, prolonged psychotherapy is not necessary or appropriate. Crisis intervention, brief treatment, support groups, and practical assistance are most effective. Mental health staff must have knowledge and skills in these modalities.

Disaster Mental Health Worker Qualifications

The disaster mental health team should be multi-disciplinary and multi-skilled. Staff should be experienced in triage, first aid, crisis intervention, and brief treatment. They should have knowledge of crisis, post-traumatic stress and grief reactions, and disaster psychology.

Survivors are often reluctant to come to mental health centers for services. Therefore, staff must be able to provide their services in non-traditional, community-based settings. Prior disaster mental health training and experience are highly recommended. In situations of mutual aid where licensed professionals cross state lines to provide assistance in disaster, licensing in the impacted state may be waived under the Good Samaritan law. This issue should be investigated in instances of cross-state mutual aid.

Staff should be well-acquainted with the functions and dynamics of the community's human service organizations and agencies (Farberow and Frederick, 1978). They should have experience in consultation and community education. Excellent communication, problem-solving, conflict resolution, and group process skills are needed, in addition to an ability to establish rapport quickly with people from diverse backgrounds.

Managers should pay careful attention to the state's scope of practice laws for various mental health professional disciplines. Individuals providing formal assessment and counseling which fall into the definition of psychotherapy should be appropriately licensed and insured for professional liability.

Qualifications For Paraprofessionals

Paraprofessionals can be excellent choices for outreach and community workers. This is especially so if they are familiar with the community and trusted by its residents. They may already be employed by a mental health, social service, health, or other community-based agency, or they may be recruited from among community residents. Characteristics and qualifications should include the following (Collins and Pancoast, 1976; Farberow and Frederick, 1978; Tierney and Baisden, 1979):

- Possess at least some high school education (to master information and concepts to be taught).
- Are indigenous to the area, if possible.
- Represent a cross section of the community/neighborhood members with regard to age, sex, ethnicity, occupation, length of residence in the community, etc.
- Are motivated to help other people, like people, and have sensitivity and empathy for others.
- Are functioning in a stable, mature, and logical manner.
- Possess sufficient emotional and physical resources and receive sufficient personal rewards to be truly capable of helping.
- Can work cooperatively with others.
- Are able to work with people of other value systems without inflicting their own value system on others.
- Are able to accept instructions and do not have ready-made, simplistic answers.
- Have an optimistic, yet realistic, view of life, i.e., a "health engendering personality".
- Have a high level of energy to remain active and resourceful in the face of stress.
- Are committed to respecting the confidentiality of survivors and are not inclined to gossip.

- Have special skills related to unique populations (e.g., children or older adults, particular ethnic groups) or useful to disaster recovery (e.g., understanding of insurance, building requirements).
- Are able to set personal limits and not become too involved with survivor recovery (e.g., understand the difference between facilitating and empowering survivors as opposed to "taking over" for the survivor).

Why Training?

Mental health professionals often assume that their clinical training and experience are more than sufficient to enable them to respond adequately in disaster. Unfortunately, traditional mental health training does not address many issues found in disaster-affected populations (FEMA, 1988). While clinical expertise, especially in the field of crisis intervention, is valuable, it is not enough. Mental health personnel need to adopt new procedures and methods for delivering a highly specialized service in disaster. Training must be designed to prepare staff for the uniqueness of disaster mental health approaches.

Though disasters profoundly affect individuals, people rarely disintegrate or become incapable of coping with the situation. Nor does mental illness suddenly manifest in a full-blown florid state. Problems do appear. They vary in nature and intensity (Farberow, 1978). However, most of the problems and post-disaster symptomatology are *normal* reactions of *normal* people to *abnormal* events. Few require traditional psychotherapy. Very few people seek out mental health assistance following disaster, and mental health staff who simply open the doors of their clinics to clients or patients will have little to do.

As a result, outreach to the community is essential. Outreach is more than simply setting up decentralized clinical services in impacted areas, or sending out brochures advertising mental health services. Outreach also means mingling with survivors in shelters and DACs and meal sites and devastated neighborhoods. The key to effective outreach is the mental health worker's ability to establish rapport and to have therapeutic intervention with individuals in an informal, social context in which there is not a psychotherapeutic "contract".

In addition to the impact on individuals, disasters are political and bureaucratic events. They profoundly affect the community and its social systems. Everyday resources for basic human needs may be destroyed or damaged. Transportation and communication may be disrupted. In a large-scale disaster, specialized emergency response and recovery agencies move into action and exert a significant influence on the post-disaster environment. Resources, structures, and individuals change as specialized response groups finish their jobs and move on and as new, grass-roots groups spring up. Mental health staff need to understand and be able to function effectively in a complex and fluid political and bureaucratic network.

Disaster mental health training will help staff to understand the impact of disaster on individuals and the community. It will provide information about the complex systems and resources in the post-disaster environment. It will also help staff to fine tune clinical skills that are relevant and useful in disaster. It will aid them in learning effective community-based approaches.

Through videotapes, role play, and other exercises, training allows staff to experience vicariously the emotional climate of disaster recovery work. Sometimes, staff may decide they are not well suited to this type of work. Usually, the experiential aspects of the training will provide workers with some measure of "emotional inoculation" that will help them to anticipate the emotional aspects of the work. Training must also provide staff with awareness of the personal impact of disaster work, and with strategies for stress management and self-care.

Before Training

It is essential for disaster mental health workers to begin to process their own emotions about the disaster before attempting to help survivors. While workers may talk about their own reactions during the training, *training is not designed to be a debriefing.* If workers come to the training with unmet needs related to their own feelings, the training will not be able to proceed effectively. A debriefing or other group format for discussion of workers' reactions to the disaster should be conducted for workers before training. A trained facilitator who has not been directly involved in service delivery, yet thoroughly understands the demands of disaster work, should provide the debriefing.

Conclusions

Disasters differ from routine emergencies in that they cannot be adequately managed merely by the mobilization of more personnel, equipment, and supplies. Disasters often create demands that exceed the capacities of single organizations. This requires them to share tasks and resources with other organizations that use unfamiliar procedures. As Auf der Heide (1989) has reported, disasters may cross jurisdictional boundaries. They change the number and structure of responding organizations, and may result in the creation of new organizations. They create new tasks, and engage participants who are not ordinarily disaster responders. Disasters also disable the routine equipment and facilities needed for emergency response.

The complexity of government in the United States compounds the difficulty in understanding "who does what" in disaster responses. The 1982 Census of Governments found over 82,000 separate governments operating in this country. This decentralization results in a lack of standardization in disaster planning and response. It complicates coordination in times of disasters (Auf der Heide, 1989).

Additionally, organizations inexperienced in disasters often respond by continuing their independent roles, failing to see how their function fits into the complex, total response effort. Auf der Heide (1989) describes this as the "Robinson Crusoe syndrome" ("We're the only ones on the island").

This isolation occurs not just in response, but also in planning. Too often, private sector groups and different levels of government may not have plans that realistically consider the roles and resources of other groups.

Due to the complexities and challenges of disaster environments, key factors in an organization's effectiveness are ***flexibility*** and the ability to ***improvise***. It is crucial, however, for responding agencies to educate themselves about the roles and responsibilities of other local, state, and federal agencies in times of disasters. They must ***plan*** for disaster response based on a solid knowledge of the organizational environment.

Comprehensive Emergency Management

In order to manage disasters efficiently and predictably, a concept called Comprehensive Emergency Management (CEM) has been developed. It applies mitigation, preparedness, response, and recovery activities to all types of hazards in a municipal/county/state/federal partnership.

Mitigation is any activity aimed at reducing or eliminating the probability of a disaster. Zoning, land use management, and public education are examples of mitigation activities. Inspection and proper maintenance of mental health facilities include fire mitigation activities.

Preparedness includes endeavors that seek to prevent casualties, expedite response activities, and minimize property damage in the event of an emergency. Pre-disaster training of a specialized mental health disaster response team is an example of preparedness activities.

Response activities occur immediately before, during, and after an emergency or disaster. Examples include search and rescue or implementation of shelter plans. Mental health response activities include providing mental health staff at shelters, first aid stations, meal sites, morgues, or command centers.

Recovery includes short and long-term activities. Short-term activities attempt initially to compensate for damage to a community's infrastructure and quickly return its vital life-support systems to operation. Short-term recovery assistance includes providing temporary housing, welfare, and unemployment assistance. Psychological first-aid, crisis intervention, and shift-change defusing (mini-debriefings) are short-term mental health recovery activities. Long-term mental health recovery activities include outreach, consultation and education, individual and group counseling, support groups and referral/information services. Both short and long-term mental health programs may be funded by a grant from the Federal Emergency Management Agency (FEMA) in a presidentially-declared disaster. The program is authorized by Section 416 of the Disaster Relief Act, Public Law 100-707 (FEMA, 1988).

Integrated Emergency Management System

The second concept which currently helps to define roles and responsibilities of emergency management is the Integrated Emergency Management System (IEMS). Drabek and Hoetmer (1991) point out that Comprehensive Emergency Management (CEM) provides an inclusive framework that encompasses all hazards and all levels of government. It includes the four phases of mitigation, preparedness, response and recovery. IEMS shows how the framework can be operationalized. It spells out the details of CEM. IEMS requires that a community carry out a hazard and risk analysis. The community then must assess its capabilities in the areas of mitigation, preparedness, response, and recovery. The shortfall between existing and required levels of capability leads to the development of a multiyear development plan. The plan usually covers a five-year period so that projects can be properly scheduled and funded, with annual work increments. Thus, IEMS supports the development of emergency management capabilities based on functions that are required for all hazards (e.g., warning, shelter, public safety, evacuation) (FEMA, 1983).

Summary

Finally, because the field of disaster mental health is highly specialized, mental health jurisdictions should have disaster plans that are thoroughly integrated with the

Comprehensive Emergency Management (CEM) plan for their jurisdiction. It is highly recommended that in a disaster of any magnitude a mental health representative with decision-making authority should be present in the Emergency Operations Center (EOC). Mental health staff play a vital role in providing stress-management functions for EOC personnel during and after EOC operations. They must be included in development of any comprehensive disaster response plan.

References

Auf der Heide, E. (1989). Disaster response: Principles of preparation and coordination. St. Louis, MO: C.V. Mosby Co.

California Department of Mental Health. (1989). California basic emergency plan. Sacramento, CA.

California Department of Mental Health. (1989). Mental health disaster plan. Sacramento, CA.

Canino, G.J.; Bravo, M.; Rubio-Stipec, M. & Woodbury, M. (1990). The impact of disaster on mental health: Prospective and retrospective analyses. *International Journal of Mental Health*, 19: 51-69.

Collins, A.H. and Pancoast, D.L. (1976). Natural helping networks: A strategy for prevention. Washington, DC: National Association of Social Workers.

Comfort, L.K. (1989). The San Salvador earthquake. In Rosenthal, U. (Ed.); Charles, M.T. (Ed.); et al *Coping with crises: The management of disasters, riots and terrorism* (pp. 323-339).

de la Fuente, R. (1990). The mental health consequences of the 1985 earthquakes in Mexico. *International Journal of Mental Health*, 19, 21-29.

DeWolfe, D. (1992). Final report: Regular grant services, Western Washington floods. State of Washington Mental Health Division.

Doherty, G.W. (1999). Cross-cultural counseling in disaster settings. *The Australasian Journal of Disaster and Trauma Studies*, Volume 1999-2

Drabek, T.E. (1985). Managing the emergency response. In Petak, W.J. "Emergency management: A challenge for public administration" (special issue). Public Administration Review 45: 85.

Drabek, T.E. and Hoetmer, G.J. (Eds.)(1991). Emergency management: Principles and practice for local government. Washington, DC: International City Management Association.

Draguns, J. G. (1975). Resocialization in culture: The complexities of taking a worldwide view of psychotherapy. In R. W. Brislin, S. Bochner, ... psycnet.apa.org/journals/amp/56/11/1019.pdf Retrieved March 6, 2010.

Federal Emergency Management Agency (1983). The Integrated Emergency Management System: Process overview. CPG 1-100. Washington, DC.

Federal Emergency Management Agency and National Institute of Mental Health. (1987). Student manual: Crisis counseling in emergency management. Washington, DC.

Federal Emergency Management Agency. (1984). Objectives for local emergency management. Washington, DC.

Federal Emergency Management Agency. (1985). National plan for federal response to a catastrophic earthquake: Basic plan (Draft 4). Washington, DC.

Federal Emergency Management Agency. (1988). Disaster assistance programs: Crisis counseling program: A handbook for grant applicants. DAP-9. Washington, DC.

Giordano, J. & Giordano, G.P. (1976). Ethnicity and community mental health. *Community Mental Health Review*, 3, 4-14, 15.

Guarnaccia, P.J. (1993). Ataques de nervios in Puerto Rico: Culture-bound syndrome or popular illness? *Medical Anthropology,* Apr, 15: 157-170.

Hartsough, D.M. and Myers, D.G. (1985). Disaster work and mental health: Prevention and control of stress among workers. Rockville, MD: National Institute of Mental Health.

Herman, R.E. (1982). Disaster planning for local government. New York: Universe Books. http://www.massey.ac.nz/~trauma/issues/1999-2/doherty.htm Retrieved March 6, 2010.

Joh, H. (1997). Disaster stress of the 1995 Kobe earthquake. *Japan Psychologia: An International Journal of Psychology in the Orient.* 40: 192-200.

Lazarus A.A. (1976). *Multimodal Behavior Therapy* Springer Publishing Co.

Lazarus, A.A. (1989). *The practice of multimodal therapy: Systematic, comprehensive and effective psychotherapy.* Johns Hopkins University.

Lazarus, A.A. (2000). Multimodal replenishment. *Professional Psychology Research and Practice,* Vol 31(1) 93-94.

Lechat, M.F. (1990). The public health dimensions of disasters. *International Journal of Mental Health,* 19: 70-79.

Lima, B.R.; Santacruz, H.; Lozano, J.: Chavez, H.; et al (1990). Disasters and mental health: Experience in Colombia and Ecuador and its relevance for primary care in mental health in Latin America. *International Journal of Mental Health,* 19: 3-20.

Marsella, A.J.; Friedman, M.J. & Gerrity, E.T. (1996). *Ethnocultural aspects of posttraumatic stress disorder: Issues, research and clinical applications.* Washington, DC, USA: American Psychological Association.

Maslow, A.H. (1987). *Motivation and personality.* (3rd. edn. rev. by R. Frager, J. Fadiman, C. McReynolds, & R. Cox). New York: Harper & Row.

Mitchell, J.T. (1983). "When disaster strikes...The critical incident stress debriefing process." Journal of Emergency Medical Services, 8:36-39.

Mitchell, J.T. and Bray, G. (1990). Emergency services stress: Guidelines for preserving the health and careers of emergency services personnel. Englewood Cliffs, NJ: Prentice-Hall, Inc.

Mitchell, J.T. and Bray, G. (1990). Emergency services stress: Guidelines for preserving the health and careers of emergency services personnel. Englewood Cliffs, NJ: Prentice-Hall, Inc.

Miura, M. & Usa, S. (1970). A psychotherapy of neurosis: Morita therapy. *Psychologia,* 13,18-34.

Myers, D. and Zunin, L. (1992). Hurricane Andrew stress management program description. Miami, FL: Federal Emergency Management Agency, Disaster Field Office 955.

Neki, J.S. (1973). Guru-chepa relationship: The possibility of a therapeutic paradigm. *American Journal of Orthopsychiatry,* 43, 755-766.

New Jersey Department of Human Services, Division of Mental Health and Hospitals (December, 1991). Responsibilities and programs manual. Newark, NJ.

Paton, D. (1996). Responding to international needs: Critical occupations as disaster relief agencies. In D. Paton & J. Violanti (Eds.). *Traumatic stress in critical occupations:*

Recognition, consequences and treatment. (pp. 139-172). Springfield, IL, USA: Charles C. Thomas, Publisher. xiv, 245 pp.

Prince, R.H. (1976). Psychotherapy as the manipulation of endogenous healing mechanisms: A transcultural survey. *Transcultural Psychiatric Research Review,* 13, 115-134.

Prince, R.H. (1980). Variations in psychotherapeutic experience. In H.C. Triandis & J.G. Draguns (Eds.), *Handbook of cross-cultural psychology. Vol 6 Psychopathology.* Boston: Allyn & Bacon.

Quarantelli, E.L. (1981). Sociobehavioral responses to chemical hazards: Preparations for and responses to acute chemical emergencies at the local community level. Newark, DE: disaster Research Center, University of Delaware.

Renteria, H. (1989, 1992). City of Oakland Office of Emergency Services.

Reynolds, D.K. (1976). *Morita psychotherapy.* Berkley: University of California Press.

Russell, P. (1991). Hospital emergency incident command system. County of Orange Health Care Agency, CA.

Santa Barbara County, California. (1991). Operational and training guide for the critical incident stress management program. Santa Barbara County Office of Emergency Services, Emergency Medical Services, and Mental Health Department. Santa Barbara, CA.

South Carolina Department of Mental Health (1991). State mental health disaster plan. Columbia, SC. .

Sue, D.W. (1977). Counseling the culturally different: A perceptual analysis. *Personnel and Guidance Journal,* 55, 422-425.

Tanaka-Matsumi, J. (1979). Cultural factors and social influence techniques in Naikan therapy: A Japanese self-observation method. *Psychotherapy: Theory, Research and Practice* 16, 385-390.

Taylor, A.J.W. (1998). Observations from a cyclone stress/trauma assignment in the Cook Islands. *Traumatology-e,* 4:1, Article 3 http://www.fsu.edu/~trauma/art3v4i1.html Retrieved March 6, 2010

Taylor, A.J.W. (1999). Towards the classification of disaster and victims. Volume 5, Issue 2 http://www.fsu.edu/~trauma/a4v5i2.html Retrieved March 6, 2010.

Taylor, A.J.W. (1999). Value conflict arising from a disaster. Australasian Journal of Disaster and Trauma Studies, Volume 1999-2 http://www.massey.ac.nc/~trauma/issues/1999-2/taylor.htm Retrieved March 6, 2010.

Taylor, A.J.W. (2000). Tragedy and trauma in Tuvalu. Australasian Journal of Disaster and Trauma Studies, Volume 2000-2 http://www.massey.ac.nc/~trauma/issues/2000-2/taylor.htm Retrieved March 6, 2010.

Tierney, K.J. and Baisden, B. (1979). Crisis intervention programs for disaster victims: A source book and manual for smaller communities. Rockville, MD: National Institute of Mental Health.

Torrey, E.F. (1972b). What western psychotherapists can learn from witchdoctors. *American Journal of Orthopsychiatry,* 42, 69-76b.

Ventura County, California. (1990). Operational and training guide for the critical incident stress management program. Ventura County Emergency Medical Services and Office of Emergency Services. Ventura, CA.

Wittkower, E.D. & Warnes, H. (1974). Cultural aspects of psychotherapy. *American Journal of Psychotherapy*, 28, 566-573.

World view of psychotherapy. In Brislin, R.W., Bochner, S. & Lonner, W.J. (Eds.), *Cross-cultural perspectives on learning.* New York: Sage Publications.

Wrenn, G.C. (1962). The culturally encapsulated counselor. *Harvard Educational Review,* 32, 444-449.

Zhang, Hou can & Zhang, Yi zhong (1991). Psychological consequences of earthquake disaster survivors. *International Journal of Psychology Special Issue: The psychological dimensions of global change*, 26, 613-621.

About the Editor

George Doherty resides in Laramie, WY where he founded the Rocky Mountain Region Disaster Mental Health Institute, Inc. He is currently employed as the President/CEO of this organization and also serves as Clinical Coordinator of the Snowy Range Critical Incident Stress Management Team. He has been involved with disaster relief since 1995, serving as a Disaster Mental Health Specialist with such incidents as the UP train wreck in Laramie, Hurricane Fran in North Carolina, the Cincinnati floods in Falmouth, KY and Tropical Storm Allison in Southeast Texas. He served as Supervisor for Disaster Mental Health for flash floods in Ft. Collins, and spent a month as the Red Cross Disaster Mental Health Coordinator for western Puerto Rico in the aftermath of Hurricane George. He has also published numerous articles in disaster mental health and traumatic stress publications and served as Guest Editor for 2 Special Editions of the journal *Traumatology* (1999 & 2004). He served as an officer in the US Air Force and was an OTS instructor, squadron commander and other positions. Additionally, he served 11 years involved in Air Search & Rescue with Civil Air Patrol in WY as Squadron Commander, Deputy Wing Commander, Air Operations Officer, and Master Observer. Certified Instructor with the Wyoming Peace Officers Standards and Training (POST). He has extensive experience conducting CISM debriefings with first responders and others and is a member of a national crisis care network, providing assistance to companies and other organizations following critical incidents involving sudden deaths and similar traumatic events.

He is a Licensed Professional Counselor in private practice and has been an adjunct instructor for a number of colleges, including Northern Nevada Community College, Warren National University and the University of Wyoming. Organizational memberships include the American Counseling Association, Voting Associate Member of the American Psychological Association, American Academy of Experts in Traumatic Stress (AETS), Association of Traumatic Stress Specialists (ATSS), Traumatic Incident Reduction Association (TIRA), Certificate of Specialized Training in the field of Mass Disaster and Terrorism, Wyoming Department of Health Emergency Preparedness Advisory Committee; Research Advisor and Research Fellow: American Biographical Institute (ABI), Editorial Advisory Board Member and Book Reviewer: *PsyCritiques* (APA Journal), Life Member of the Air Force Association, and Life Member of the Military Officers Association of America, Life Member: Pennsylvania State University Alumni Association, Alumni Admissions Volunteer - Pennsylvania State University.

Publications include: *Crisis Intervention Training for Disaster Workers: An Introduction.*; Editor and contributor for the *Proceedings of Rocky Mountain Region Disaster Mental Health Conferences* (2005, 2006, 2007, 2008). Served as Guest Editor for Special issues of the journal *Traumatology* on Disaster Mental Health (1999) and Crises in Rural America (2004); .Cross-cultural Counseling in Disaster Settings. - *Austral-Asian Journal of Disaster and Trauma Studies* (1999). Published reviews include: Understanding Oslo in Troubled Times; Responders to September 11, 2001: Counseling: Innovative Responses to 9/11 Firefighters, Families, and

Communities; Genocide: A Human Condition? Stress Management, Wellness and Organizational Health., .Leadership Competency and Conflict.; Leadership: Lessons from the Ancient World - all in *PsyCritiques*. Conference Director for annual Rocky Mountain Disaster Mental Health Conferences 1999 -present.

Additional past positions include: Masters Level Psychologist – Rural Clinics (State of Nevada), 1980 – 1986; Veterans Counselor (VA Contract) – 1980-1986, NV; Counselor – pre-delinquent children and families – CORA Services (Philadelphia, PA).1972-1975; Program Coordinator - Community Action Programs (EOAC, Office of Economic Opportunity – Waco/McLennan County, TX) 1968-1971.

Summaries of Additional Presentations

The 8th Rocky Mountain Region Disaster Mental Health Conference in Cheyenne, Wyoming in November, 2009 included a large number of presentations. Papers or articles were submitted by most, including invited papers from international specialists. However, in an attempt to make these proceedings more complete, summaries are presented below for those few without papers.

- **"Emotional Responses to a Flood: The response of North Dakota's volunteer organizations."** Art Storey, Voluntary Agency Liaison, FEMA Region 8.

  This presentation discussed what several North Dakota volunteer organizations did and are doing with emotional care after the spring and summer 2009 storms in their state. It shared some of the challenges and issues presented to them as a result of a disaster that lasted from March until August. They did it without a request and therefore no federal money available for crisis counseling through a federal Crisis Counseling grant. Some of the emotional needs included suicides that occurred as a result of some of the stress on disaster victims.

  It addressed the training that was done for Disaster Case Managers (mostly volunteers) and for leaders of faith based (mostly churches) leaders as they tried to deal with the stress and emotional needs that resulted in an almost 4 month long disaster. It presented and discussed the challenges and success that they achieved with the training. The presentation included some of the materials developed by these groups as well as the issues that they faced and continue to face.

  The presenter also explained how a state can apply for and receive a Crisis Counseling Grant after a federally declared disaster and what those funds can pay for.

  - **Biographical Statement** – Art Storey is the Voluntary Liaison for FEMA Region 8 which includes the states of Wyoming, Montana, Colorado, Utah, North Dakota and South Dakota. He has been in this position for the past 8 years. In this position he has responded to more than 21 declared and 11 non-declared disasters in 18 states including the 9-11 attack in New York and Katrina in Louisiana. He served with the Salvation Army for 20 years in many assignments throughout the Western United States including the Territorial Disaster Coordinator for the Western Territory extending from Alaska to Guam and from Texas to the Canadian border. Also was a Deputy Sheriff for Los Angeles County including corrections, patrol and a SWAT team member.

- **"Disaster Preparedness in the Wild, Wild, West....Y.O.Y.O."** Constance E. Sweeney, R.N., B.S.

  This presentation encouraged participants to look beyond the usual flashlights, food supplies, and water storage that most disaster manuals cover. It got to the practical matters of caring for the sick and injured, disabled, or special needs populations. The topics covered were aimed at helping the frontier community residents be self-sufficient and care for themselves when health resources are limited or nonexistent.

  - **Biographical Statement:** Connie has been in nursing since before they walked on the moon. She is currently employed by WDH\Lincoln County Public Health in Kemmerer, Wyoming. Connie was a member in the Girl Scouts. As GSA's motto dictates, she is always prepared and has been interested in disaster preparedness since volunteering at an evacuation center in her hometown when she was a teenager. Even though most of Connie's training was in Maternal/Child Health, she stayed involved with emergency management and disaster planning. Connie has a husband, two children and four grandchildren. She loves camping, hockey, wildlife and old west history.

- **"Aging Trends in Wyoming, Are you ready for the future?"** Timothy Ernst, Community Program Manager, Aging Division, Wyoming Department of Health This presentation gave the participant a look into the future trends of Wyoming Aging and Disabled population and what to expect should a disaster of any type happen.

  - **Biographical Statement:** Tim Ernst is a program manager for the Wyoming Department of Health, Aging Division in Cheyenne, Wyoming. Tim has been with the Aging Division since 2001 and oversees the Community Based In-Home Services Program. Tim has been designated, by the Administration on Aging (AoA) region VIII, to be the State of Wyoming, Aging Division's disaster point person. Tim draws from his experience from being an emergency medical technician for the Carbon County EMS for 13 plus years and being the interim executive director for the Governor's Planning Council on Developmental Disabilities.

- **"National Guard Family Services Program: Wyoming Family Assistance Centers"**

  Compiled by Debbie Russell, Specialist with the Wyoming Family Assistance Program (FAC) And Daniella Hamilton, Representative with the Wyoming Family Assistance Program

  Biographical Statements:

  - **Debbie Russell** is a Specialist with the Wyoming Family Assistance Program (FAC). She supervises and trains the Family Assistance Center Representatives and assists in training the Lead Volunteers. Debbie Russell began working with the Family Program in 1987 as a volunteer and then accepted the position as the FAC Supervisor in 2003. Being a parent and spouse of a service member for 26 years, she recognizes the need for providing assistance to families before, during and after deployment.

- **Daniella Hamilton** is a representative with the Wyoming Family Assistance Program. She accepted a position with the Family Assistance Center in 2003 when her husband was deployed. Daniella currently is in charge of the Central Region and the Northeastern Region of the state. Being a spouse of a Military member for 16 years has helped her in understanding and assisting others with the challenges they face in military life.

♦ **Treatment of PTSD with a right brain model in an experiential setting** Jamie Egolf MSW, LCSW, Jungian Psychotherapist and Chavawn Kelly, MA, Writer

The method of dramatic reenactment (theatre) and authentic witnessing (poetry) presented here by the presenters was created for the purpose of training responders, counselors, and others who work with persons traumatized by war, natural disaster, sudden death or other tragedies or to work directly with trauma victims. The presenters created the method to treat trauma using techniques that elevate trauma to the imaginal level, thereby allowing new neural pathways to be created. Although the memory of the trauma will remain, the goal of treatment is for the all-consuming pain to subside, therefore allowing the participant to begin the healing process and pursue a healthy life.

Authentic witnessing is a significant component of the treatment because both the traumatized person and the situation are acknowledged by empathic practitioners and participants who are engaged in the treatment. To heal from trauma, victims must deal with emotion and image above all and "stand beside themselves" in an ecstatic" observation. Only then can new neural pathways be forged. The art that is created not only stands in witness of the individual and the traumatic event but also as an external vessel that may hold a portion of the traumatized person's pain.

- **Biographical Statements:**

Jamie Egolf is a Jungian Psychotherapist and Consultant, in practice for 38 years, now practices in Laramie, Wyoming, received the MSW at Catholic University of America, Washington, DC; studied art at Purdue University; was trained by the Interregional Society of Jungian Analysts; and in Psychodrama and Creative Writing. She began *The Magic Theatre of Life* (workshops in psychodrama and drama therapy,) co-authored the *Pre-Marital Inventory*; presented *Dreaming Superman* at the University of Melbourne's *Superhero Conference, 2005, published in Superheroes: From Hercules to Superman* by New Academia Press in 2007; *presented Desire and Sensuality in the Music and Relationships of Claude Debussy: A Look at the Split in the* Archetypal Feminine at the 2007 Creativity and Madness *Conference* in Santa Fe with Pianist Gary Smart. She *presented Geysers, Grizzlies, and Paint Pots: Finding the Deep Self in the Yellowstone/ Wyoming Wilderness and the Wilderness of the Psyche* at the Foundation for Mythological *Studies Nature and Human Nature Conference, 2007.* Accepted for publication: *Flyboy's Daughter* was presented at the 2007 Disaster Mental Health Conference (conference proceedings have subsequently been published). Her paper *Image, Symbol, and Story in*

The Medieval and Contemporary Tapestry and the Comic Strip was presented at the San Francisco Jung Institute's *Art and Psyche* Conference in May, 2008.

Chavawn Kelley has spent her career exploring questions of effective communication. She is the corporate communications manager for Western Research Institute in Laramie, Wyoming. She earned her Master of Arts degree in American Studies from the University of Wyoming and has given presentations for the Wyoming Humanities Council throughout the state since 2004. Her short stories, essays and poems have been published in literary journals, and she has been awarded fellowships and grants from the Wyoming Arts Council, the Wyoming Historical Society, the Ucross Foundation, the Ludwig Vogelstein Foundation, and Can Serrat International Arts Center.

- **"Organizations that focus on helping the Veteran, their families and community heal from the effects of War: Give an Hour, Soldier's Heart, Vet Art Project, FF4Vets and Families."** Michelle A. Worden, MS, NCC, LPC

Give An Hour is asking mental health professionals nationwide to literally give an hour of their time each week to provide free mental health services to military personnel and their families. Target population is the U.S. troops and families who are being affected by the current military conflicts in Afghanistan and Iraq.

- **BIOGRAPHICAL STATEMENT: Michelle A Worden, Licensed Professional Counselor,** in private practice in Laramie Wyoming. She has dedicated much of her professional service to Veterans and their families: focusing on helping them heal from trauma, substance abuse and isolation. She also is working on helping create a more correct and rightful relationship between community members and Veterans. She does this by organizing safe spaces and events for Veterans to share their stories and for the community to bear witness and share in the burden. Along with involvement with Give an Hour in which she donates an hour a week of counseling service to a service member or their family or close friends; she is also involved with other national nonprofit organizations like Soldiers Heart—a Veteran healing project that provides healing retreats, community trainings and support. Vet Art project—a Veteran art and storytelling project based out of Chicago that helps Veterans and their loved ones use many art modalities to share their experiences. Lastly she supports a local Laramie group called Fire Fighters 4 Vets and Families created and lead by DC Faber (an Afghanistan Veteran) - a monthly group that connects Veterans, family and community and gives them a safe place to meet and share their experiences and to serve—-to aid in doing a better job welcoming our service members home; mind/body/spirit.

- **"All Hazards on the Wind River Indian Reservation**," Dan O'Leary, DVM, DACVPM, Field Epidemiology Officer, Wyoming Department of Health Public Health and Emergency Preparedness Program

Wyoming State Health Department's Public Health and Terrorism Preparedness program continues building strong collaborative ties with Wyoming's Northern Arapaho and Eastern Shoshone tribes residing on the Wind River Indian Reservation (WRIR). The platform for this collaboration is the Wind River All Hazards Steering Committee comprised of tribal, local, state, and federal partners. The Committee meets monthly to bi-monthly on WRIR, vested by tribal leaders with authority to identify and assign resources to WRIR's public health preparedness needs. This presentation highlighted the Committee's broad array of projects, accomplishments, and challenges in building public health preparedness on WRIR.

- **BIOGRAPHICAL STATEMENT: Dan O'Leary, DVM, DACVPM**

May, 2006-present: US Centers for Disease Control and Prevention (CDC) Career Epidemiology Field Officer, Wyoming Department of Health Public Health Emergency Preparedness program. Focus: tribal public health emergency preparedness.

In 2002-2006: Senior epidemiologist, CDC Division of Vector-Borne Infectious Diseases, Fort Collins, CO. Focus: epidemiology and national surveillance of West Nile virus and other arthropod-borne viruses.

2000-2002: CDC chronic disease epidemiology field assignee, South Dakota Department of Health. Focus: diabetes and smoking prevention.

2001: Board Certification, American College of Veterinary Preventive Medicine.

1998-2000: CDC Epidemic Intelligence Service (EIS) Fellow, Division of Vector-Borne Infectious Diseases, Fort Collins, CO. Focus: epidemiology and prevention of Lyme disease, plague, tularemia, relapsing fever, dengue, and West Nile virus.

1993-1998: US Air Force public health officer; duty stations in Omaha, NE and Rapid City, SD. Focus: public health preventive medicine.

1988-1993: Veterinary private practice, CO and MD. Focus: equine and small animal medicine and surgery.

1988: Doctor of Veterinary Medicine, University of Wisconsin School of Veterinary Medicine

1983: Bachelor of Science Wildlife and Fisheries Management, Frostburg State College, MD

"Post-beetle Outbreak Wildfire: What, really, are the real threats?" Duane Short, Biodiversity Conservation Alliance's (BCA) Wild Species Program Director and primary forest defense staffer for the Medicine Bow National Forest.

Duane Short offered a review of the best and most recently available scientific studies that investigate factors likely to have the most influence on the character (scope, intensity and spread rate) of post-beetle kill wildfires in the Medicine Bow National Forest and surrounding forested landscapes.

Fact and myth regarding the predictions of catastrophic wildfire were distinguished, where possible, and potential fact/myth gray areas were discussed.

- **Biographical Statement:** Duane writes detailed comments and appeals on projects that threaten forest health, oversees the drafting of Endangered Species petitions and litigation, and works closely with the media. Duane holds a Bachelor of Science degree in Zoology from Northern Arizona University, is a professional writer and possesses nearly 20 years of conservation advocacy experience. Earlier in life he served as a volunteer firefighter in his southern Illinois hometown. Following his formal education he taught the core sciences curriculum in (what was at the time) the nation's only accelerated respiratory therapy program (South West Academy of Technology, Mesa Arizona), performed American Association of Sleep Technologists certified sleep studies (Polysomnography) and provided Intraoperative Monitoring (IOM) procedures for neurosurgeons as they conducted spinal surgeries.

  Duane's lifelong love for nature and its complex processes finally won out later in his life compelling him to volunteer untold hours toward environmental protection and conservation efforts. Long story short, Short is soon entering his fourth year with BCA. He is noted for his passion for science and an understanding and appreciation for nature that continual learning fosters.

About The Rocky Mountain Region Disaster Mental Health Institute

Mission:

The Rocky Mountain Region Disaster Mental Health Institute is an independent, nonprofit, 501(c) (3) corporation whose mission is to promote the development and application of practice, research, and training in disaster mental health, Critical Incident Stress Management, traumatology and other emergency response interventions and the promotion of community awareness, resilience and recovery. This includes hazards vulnerability and mitigation research, planning and training for first responders, mental health professionals, chaplains and related personnel.

Purpose:

The purpose of the Institute is to provide a forum for presentation of research results, education, training and consultation in Disaster Mental Health Services (DMHS) and Critical Incident Stress Management (CISD/CISM), advances in delivery of DMHS and CISD/CISM, discussion and sharing of information, ideas and plans, development of a DMHS and CISD/CISM research and service delivery network, presentation of Continuing Education training for mental health professionals, first responders and chaplains, training for newly recruited DMHS and CISD/CISM volunteers and first responders, and publication of program proceedings and papers as appropriate for dissemination to DMHS and CISD/CISM professionals and first responders locally, regionally and nationally.

Significance:

Mental Health Services before, during and following disasters, critical incidents, crises, and terrorist activities are becoming an integral part of disaster and critical incident preparedness, mitigation, response, and follow-up. Disaster Mental Health Services is a relatively new field which has expanded significantly within the past ten years. Critical Incident Stress Debriefing and Critical Incident Stress Management have been around since the early 1980s. In order to continue to grow and meet identified needs, both will require continued development as well as focused research and training. Research will help identify how Mental Health Services can best be utilized as well as how relevant changes need to be made in practice. Networking and sharing experiences can also help develop resources.

The long-term goal includes training emergency Disaster Mental Health teams and CISM teams to conduct interventions for corporations, states, municipalities and rural communities in the Rocky Mountain region and to evaluate their effectiveness in reducing the effects of trauma on first responders and others as well as affected communities and organizations.

Who Should Attend

The conference is a must experience for anyone working in the fields of: emergency medical services and trauma units, crisis intervention, mental health, traumatic stress, emergency services, disaster mental health, military, National Guard & Reserve, schools, law enforcement, firefighters, chaplains and other first responders.

Certificates of Attendance

All conference delegates will be provided with Certificates of Attendance. Each presentation will be listed on the reverse with the number of contact hours. It is the responsibility of the delegate to have each presenter sign off on their certificate. Your Certificate of Attendance will be printed with your name exactly as it appears on your Registration form. Please make sure that you print it clearly. A small fee of $5.00 will be assessed to make and mail a duplicate certificate. If you register late or onsite, your certificate will be printed and mailed approximately 3 weeks post-conference.

ROCKY MOUNTAIN REGION DISASTER MENTAL HEALTH INSTITUTE
PO BOX 786
LARAMIE, WY 82073-0786

http://www.rmrinstitute.org/rocky.html
email: rockymountain@mail2emergency.com
Phone: 307-399-4818

The Rocky Mountain Region Disaster Mental Health Institute is a 501(c)3 Non-profit Organization.

Index

SOCIAL SCIENCE / Disasters & Disaster Relief **US$24.95/£12.95**

Proceedings of the 5th Rocky Mountain Region Disaster Mental Health Conference

Recent years have seen an extraordinary number of major disasters, critical incidents and other events that have had major impacts on our world. The 2004 tsunami, hurricanes Rita and Katrina, and the wars in Iraq and Afghanistan affect millions of lives daily. Potential events such as Avian Flu pandemic, global warming and the increasing threats of spreading unrest in the Middle East are concerns that weigh heavily on us all.

November 8-11, 2006, the Rocky Mountain Region Disaster Mental Health Institute held their Annual four-day Disaster Mental Health Conference. The theme of the conference was **Taking Charge In Troubled Times: Response, Resilience, Recovery and Follow-up**. This edition contains the major papers presented at the conference and summaries of additional presentations. They address some of the major crisis events confronting our societies in recent years, namely, large disasters such as hurricanes Katrina and Rita; case studies such as Abu Ghraib, and traumatic events such as a night club suicide bombing, the role of cultural sensitivity and ethics in disaster settings, resilience, and the importance of planning, education and taking care of our first responders and mental health professionals. An additional concern with information includes information about preparation of communities and families for deployment and return of military personnel. The importance of planning for how mental health personnel can respond in the event of an Avian Flu Pandemic is also discussed. Presenters are drawn from researchers and responders from Wyoming, the United States, and the United Kingdom.

"This compilation of 10 papers deals with people's reactions to a wide variety of disasters, including not only terror and Hurricane Katrina, but child abuse and the trauma suffered by families of service members. Taken together, the papers are fascinating. The "Proceedings of the 5th Rocky Mountain Region Disaster Mental Health Conference" provides insight into the nature of the individual's response to terror and disaster. They should be interesting reading for everyone who either indirectly or directly has been affected."

—Linda Benninghoff, Reader Views

SOCIAL SCIENCE / Disasters & Disaster Relief **US$24.95/£12.95**

Proceedings of the 6th Rocky Mountain Region Disaster Mental Health Conference

Events around the world continue to present challenges for first responders and mental health professionals. Natural and man-made disasters continue. Evidence mounts concerning potential events such as global warming and the effects this may have worldwide. Avian Flu remains a concern as do forms of biological terrorism and natural hazards such as tsunamis, floods, hurricanes and earthquakes. The 2004 tsunami in Sri Lanka and Thailand continues to have a significant impact on that area of the world. Wars in Afghanistan and Iraq continue to impact those countries, the Middle East and the United States. Preparing our communities and families not only for deployments and support of those deployed and their families, but also for the aftermath and return of our military and National Guard personnel into our communities is important for all.

What can we expect from all of these? How do communities and first responders handle these? What role does mental health play? How do first responders and mental health professionals plan together for responding to future events and learning from past ones. Using a strategic planning approach, how do we identity potential threats and identify target populations and groups? What resources are available for which identified threats? How do we do such planning, how often, and how do we exercise such plans prior to events? What can we learn from such events and how do we incorporate what we learn into future planning?

It is crucial that response, resilience, recovery and follow-up be included in our planning. Additional variables important in responding include cultural knowledge and sensitivity. We need to prepare to respond appropriately within a culture not our own, whether locally, nationally, or internationally.

November 8-10, 2007, the Rocky Mountain Region Disaster Mental Health Institute held their Annual Disaster Mental Health Conference in Cheyenne, Wyoming. The theme of this conference was: **From Crisis To Recovery: Resilience and Strategic Planning for the Future**.

"*Proceedings of the 6th Rocky Mountain Region Disaster Mental Health Conference* is a must have for first responders and mental health professionals. Addressing the needs of people who work in these fields is critical. The better trained they are to be emotionally equipped for disasters, the better they can help others. I think that the 120 pages of information covered in this book will be some of the most important information needed by people in this field today."

—Page Lovitt, *Reader Views*

Social Science: Disasters & Disaster Relief **US $29.95 / £ 14.95**

Crisis Intervention Training for Disaster Workers

George W. Doherty, MS, LPC

This book provides information about training for mental health professionals and first responders who work with victims of disaster related stress and trauma. It helps prepare them to relate with disaster victims and co-workers. Warning signs and symptoms are explored together with stages, strategies and interventions for recovery.

The book will introduce you to disasters, the community response, the roles of first responders, Disaster Mental Health Services and Critical Incident Stress Management (CISM) responders and teams. It provides a brief overview of these and their roles in responding to the needs of both victims and disaster workers. The role of CISM is presented and discussed both for disasters and other critical incidents. This includes discussion about war, terrorism and follow-up responses by mental health professionals. The book is designed to help readers identify appropriate methods for activating Disaster Mental Health Crisis Intervention Teams for disaster mental health services for victims, co-workers, and self.

The content includes general theory and models of Disaster Mental Health, CISM, crisis intervention techniques commonly used in these situations, supportive research, and practice of approaches used in responding to the victims, workers and communities affected by disasters, critical incidents and terrorism threats and events.

"Provides a breadth and depth of knowledge as well as practical tools for beginner to expert. Should be required reading for all disaster responders, and, especially, mental health professionals considering disaster work."

—Bruce L. Andrews, MS, LPC (ARC Disaster Mental Provider/Instructor)

"This text serves as a wonderful adjunct and lead into the discipline of CISM. It provides a brief survey of disaster mental health and disaster mental health services."

—Thomas Mitchell, LPC

Rocky Mountain
Disaster Mental Health Institute
Press

"Learning from the past and planning for the future"

RMRInstitute.org

Special Offers

Order Direct from the Publisher and Save on Disaster Mental Health Titles!

Order Form – 25% Discount Off List Price!

Ship To:

☐ VISA ☐ MasterCard ☐ American Express ☐ check payable to **Loving Healing Press**

Name ______

Address ______ Card # ______ Expires ___/___

Address ______ Signature ______

City ______ State ______

District Country Zip/Post code ______

Daytime phone # ______

email address ______

RMR Proceedings #6	____	x $18.95 =	____
RMR Proceedings #7	____	x $22.95 =	____
RMR Proceedings #8	____	x $20.95 =	____
Crisis Intervention Training...	____	x $22.95 =	____
		Subtotal =	____
		Michigan Residents: 6% tax =	____
		Shipping charge (see below)	____
		Your Total	$____

Shipping price per copy via:

☐ USA only MediaMail (+ $3) ☐ USA Priority Mail (+ $4) ☐ Int'l Airmail (+ $5)

Fax Order Form back to (734)663-6861 or

Mail to LHP, 5145 Pontiac Trail, Ann Arbor, MI 48105

www.ingramcontent.com/pod-product-compliance
Ingram Content Group UK Ltd.
Pitfield, Milton Keynes, MK11 3LW, UK
UKHW050614260726
13967UKWH00008B/2867

9 781615 990399